MW01635055

Training for Victory

Training for Victory

The British Commonwealth Air Training Plan in the West

Peter C. Conrad

Western Producer Prairie Books
Saskatoon, Saskatchewan

Western Producer Prairie Books
Saskatoon, Saskatchewan

5 4 3 2 1

Cover photograph courtesy Western Canada Pictorial Index
Cover design by John Luckhurst/GDL
Interior design by Pendleton Penner Advertising Incorporated, Saskatoon

Printed and bound in Canada

The publisher acknowledges the support received for this publication from the Canada Council.

Western Producer Prairie Books is a unique publishing venture located in the middle of western Canada and owned by a group of prairie farmers who are members of Saskatchewan Wheat Pool. From the first book in 1954, a reprint of a serial originally carried in the weekly newspaper *The Western Producer*, to the book before you now, the tradition of providing enjoyable and informative reading for all Canadians is continued.

Canadian Cataloguing in Publication Data

Conrad, Peter C. (Peter Christopher)
Training for victory : the British Commonwealth
Air Training Plan in the West

Includes bibliographical references.
ISBN: 0–88833–302–1

1. British Commonwealth Air Training Plan. 2. World War, 1939–1945 – Prairie Provinces. 3. World War, 1939–1945 – Aerial operations, Canadian. 4. World War, 1939–1945 – Aerial operations. I. Title.
UG639.C2C657 1989 940.54/4971 C89–098132–9

To the person
who made this work
possible

Marilyn
Simonne

Contents

Preface ... ix

Acknowledgements ... xi

Maps ... xii

CHAPTER 1
Canada Becomes the Centre for Training Aircrew ... 1

CHAPTER 2
Preparing for the Great Undertaking ... 8

CHAPTER 3
Building for the Future ... 14

CHAPTER 4
For Duty and Prosperity ... 18

CHAPTER 5
"Cheered in the Streets" ... 23

CHAPTER 6
Going Through the Mill ... 27

CHAPTER 7
Hazards of War ... 37

CHAPTER 8
Operating the Plan ... 41

CHAPTER 9
"The Tie that Binds" ... 49

CHAPTER 10
Sharing Field and Ice ... 61

CHAPTER 11
Zoot-Suiters and the Yellow Bellied ... 68

CHAPTER 12
A Crisis of its Own ... 73

CHAPTER 13
Mackenzie King, Diefenbaker, and the Struggle for a School ... 83

CHAPTER 14
The Plan's Aviation Legacy ... 90

Notes ... 93

Index ... 101

Preface

There was nothing different about the field of prairie grass that I stood in except that in the distance there were huge grey buildings that looked like a set for a World War Two movie. But, looking at the scene more closely, it was clear that the dark buildings were in a state of disrepair and that the grass I stood on was growing through cracks in what had once been runways. In this field, as in many others across the Prairies, the remains of the Jacob, Wright, and huge Pratt and Whitney engines that once roared through the skies of the Canadian West lay in the deep grass, only rusting memories of a massive national effort.

The eerie summer scene was at Vulcan, Alberta. The buildings were from the instructor flying school and service flying training school of the British Commonwealth Air Training Plan, which had trained massive numbers of aircrew for the Allied cause. The final number of trained personnel was over 131,000 at a cost in excess of two and a quarter billion dollars.

When doing the research for this book, I was struck by two realities of the Air Training Plan. The first was its magnitude. Air schools were located across the country. Indeed, the BCATP was a central focus of the nation during the war. The second was the high level of uniformity among the schools located in British Columbia, the Prairies, Ontario, Quebec, and the Maritimes. From interviews with those who were involved in the Plan, it was clear that there were few differences between the schools regardless of where they were across Canada.

Although there was uniformity in the way that the schools operated and in the way they related to the communities around them, the Prairies as a region experienced especially significant changes as a result of its involvement. The Prairies had just been liberated from the Great Depression in the late 1930s. The economic prosperity that accompanied the schools aided in the recovery, and, at the same time, began to ease the feeling among western Canadians of being alienated from eastern Canada, a feeling that had been aggravated by the Depression. Approximately half the air training schools of the Plan were located in the Prairies, making the region an important part of the national war effort. The experience of being an equal partner in a national effort brought about a decline in western Canadian alienation during the war years that continued in the postwar era.

I would like to thank those who sent letters to help in the research of this book. I am also grateful to those who invited me into their homes to be interviewed. A special thanks to Bill and Dorothy Minor, Stan Frith, Ken Melby, Don O'Hearn, Mr. Edger, Jim Brooks, Eva Frith, Fred Hawkins, Harald Marfell, Harry Riviere, Yvonne S. Bergess, Mrs. Ethel Holderbein, Gordon Chappell, Dunc Campbell, John Schultz, Mr. E. J. Anderson, Mrs. J. R. Hamilton, Ken Brown, W. A. Gordon, Robert. N. Brown, Jack Kerr, Jack Park, Mr. E. W. D. Cannon, Mr. Donald Couch, Thelma Bone, N. K. Leatherdale, William F. Fowler, A. H. Clark, Dalton Deedrick, Bill Hemstreet, John Wing, Roland (Rollie) Wilkes, Ken and Dorothy Currie, W. Paul Heasman, Phil Ellison, C. A. (Smoky) Robson, Pat Coggins, Stan Morris, and Robert Steel.

A special thanks also to Jim Kirk, who wrote letters, agreed to an interview, and took late night phone calls.

I am grateful for the help I received in the early phases of the study from Dr. W. A. Waiser at the University of Saskatchewan.

I would also like to thank Warren Clubb at the Saskatoon branch of the Western Development Museum for his assistance.

In addition, I would like to thank Virginia Hatch-Stewart at the Moose Jaw branch of the Western Development Museum for allowing me to use Fred Hatch's papers.

I am grateful to the J. S. Ewart Fund of the University of Manitoba which financed a research trip to Ottawa.

I also received valuable editing and suggestions from Dave Margoshes. Any errors of fact or interpretation are my own.

A special thanks to my wife, Marilyn, for all the help, support and encouragement she gave me.

BRITISH COMMONWEALTH AIR TRAINING PLAN
PILOT TRAINING FACILITIES IN THE WEST
1940-1945

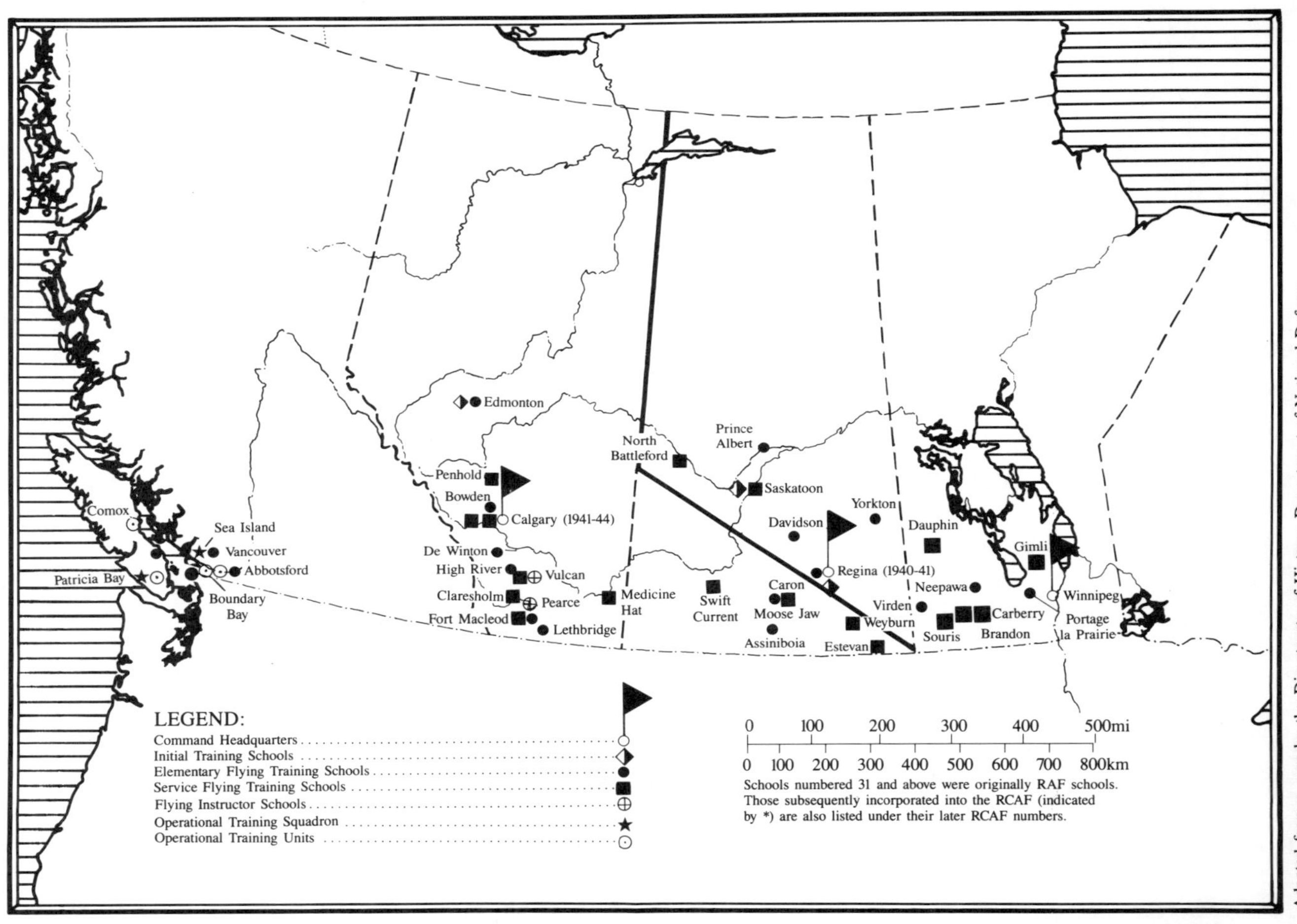

Adapted from a map by the Directorate of History, Department of National Defence. Reproduced with the permission of the Minister of Supply and Services Canada, 1989.

NO. 4 TRAINING COMMAND
HEADQUARTERS, REGINA/CALGARY

Initial Training Schools
- No. 2 Regina
- No. 4 Edmonton

Elementary Flying Training Schools
- No. 5 Lethbridge (moved to High River June 1941)
- No. 8 Vancouver
- No. 15 Regina
- No. 16 Edmonton
- No. 18 Boundary Bay
- No. 24 Abbotsford
- No. 25 Assiniboia
- No. 31 De Winton
- No. 32 Bowden
- No. 33 Caron
- *No. 34 Assiniboia
- No. 36 Pearce

Service Flying Training Schools
- No. 3 Calgary
- No. 7 Fort Macleod
- No. 8 Weyburn
- No. 15 Claresholm
- No. 19 Vulcan
- No. 32 Moose Jaw
- No. 34 Medicine Hat
- No. 36 Penhold
- No. 37 Calgary
- No. 38 Estevan
- No. 39 Swift Current
- *No. 41 Weyburn

Flying Instructor School
- No. 2 Vulcan (moved to Pearce May 1943)

Operational Training Squadron (WAC)
- No. 13 Sea Island (moved to Patricia Bay November 1940)

Operational Training Units (WAC)
- No. 3 Patricia Bay
- No. 5 Boundary Bay (Det. at Abbotsford from August 1944)
- No. 6 Comox
- *No. 32 Patricia Bay

NO. 2 TRAINING COMMAND
HEADQUARTERS, WINNIPEG

Initial Training School
- No. 7 Saskatoon

Elementary Flying Training Schools
- No. 2 Fort William
- No. 6 Prince Albert
- No. 14 Portage la Prairie
- No. 19 Virden
- No. 23 Davidson (moved to Yorkton January 1945)
- No. 26 Neepawa
- *No. 35 Neepawa

Service Flying Training Schools
- No. 4 Saskatoon
- No. 10 Dauphin
- No. 11 Yorkton
- No. 12 Brandon
- No. 13 North Battleford
- No. 17 Souris
- No. 18 Gimli
- No. 33 Carberry
- *No. 35 North Battleford

BRITISH COMMONWEALTH AIR TRAINING PLAN
AIRCREW (OTHER THAN PILOT) TRAINING FACILITIES IN THE WEST
1940-1945

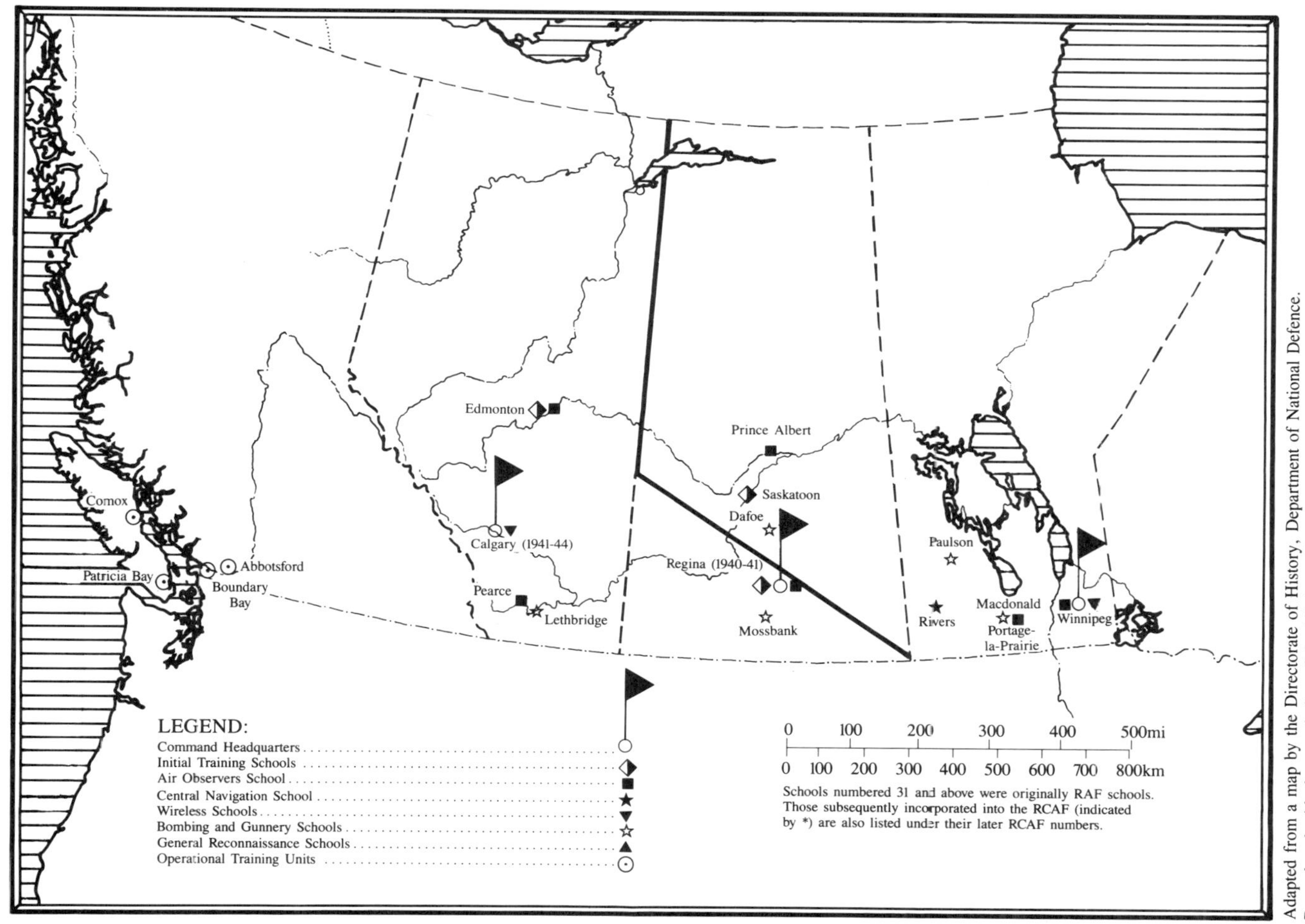

Adapted from a map by the Directorate of History, Department of National Defence. Reproduced with the permission of the Minister of Supply and Services Canada, 1989.

NO. 4 TRAINING COMMAND
HEADQUARTERS, REGINA/CALGARY

Initial Training Schools
- No. 2 Regina
- No. 4 Edmonton

Air Observers Schools
- No. 2 Edmonton
- No. 3 Regina (moved to Pearce September 1942)

Wireless School
- No. 2 Calgary

Bombing and Gunnery Schools
- No. 2 Mossbank
- No. 8 Lethbridge

Operational Training Units (WAC)
- No. 3 Patricia Bay
- No. 5 Boundary Bay (Det. at Abbotsford from August 1944)
- No. 6 Comox
- *No. 32 Patricia Bay

NO. 2 TRAINING COMMAND
HEADQUARTERS, WINNIPEG

Initial Training School
- No. 7 Saskatoon

Air Observers Schools
- No. 5 Winnipeg
- No. 6 Prince Albert
- No. 7 Portage la Prairie

Central Navigation School
- No. 1 Rivers

Wireless School
- No. 3 Winnipeg

Bombing and Gunnery Schools
- No. 3 Macdonald
- No. 5 Dafoe
- No. 7 Paulson

1

Canada Becomes the Centre for Training Aircrew

After long difficult negotiations between New Zealand, Australia, Britain, and Canada, the agreement that brought the British Commonwealth Air Training Plan into being was to be signed on December 16, 1939, over three months after the Second World War had broken out. With the final agreement before Prime Minister William Lyon Mackenzie King, the British delegation was summoned to his office late in the day. The delegations from New Zealand and Australia had already left Canada and would have to sign the document later.

Mackenzie King greeted the British delegation as the hands of the clock ticked past midnight. The prime minister remarked that December 17 was his birthday. After he received a round of congratulations, King said there was one small issue that had to be resolved: the date on the document they had gathered to sign was December 16, but, at the moment of the signing, it was December 17. King thought that the agreement would be luckier if it was signed and dated on his birthday. After a moment of consideration, the British delegation agreed to the change. With the date changed to December 17, 1939, the Air Training Plan came into existence.[1]

Fifty years after the signing of an agreement that made Canada the most significant centre for air training during the Second World War, few Canadians know about it. Fewer know why Canada became the centre for air training for the Allies. Many would be surprised to know that Canada was already highly respected as an air training centre on the eve of the Second World War.

Private Schools for Fighter Pilots

Canada's air training history began in the Great War. From the very beginning of the Great War, Canadians were active in supplying trained aircrew to the Allied cause as businesses built private schools for those who wished to train for one of the two flying services of Great Britain.

Any Canadian interested in joining the Royal Flying Corps or the Royal Naval Air Corps in 1914 and 1915 had to go to the regular recruitment centres of the Canadian Expeditionary Forces, ask for a transfer to the flying service of their choice, and hope for the best. Often this led to service in the trenches of France instead of the skies overhead. The only way anyone could be assured of easy entry into the flying services was to already be a trained pilot.[2]

In Canada in 1915 there were only two places to obtain pilot training: the Curtiss Aviation School in Toronto, or the Aero Club of British Columbia (which became the British Columbia Aviation School late in 1915) in Vancouver.

The Royal Flying Corps Comes to Canada

To meet the need for large numbers of pilots, more money, government support, and organization of recruitment and training was called for in 1917. The need was fulfilled that year when the Royal Flying Corps arrived in Canada to establish a school, the same year it established a school in Egypt.

The Canadian government supported the training project, but the commander in charge was responsible only to the War Office and later to the Air Ministry in London.[3]

The Canadian air training program of the Great War was very successful. Of 9,200 cadets who enlisted, 3,135 completed their pilot training. Over 2,500 pilots went overseas. The remainder were either instructors or were waiting to be transported when the Armistice was signed. Of the pilots who went overseas, 838 were killed. As well, 137 air observers were trained and 85 were sent overseas.[4]

The Birth of the RCAF

The different military offices in Canada were unified into the Department of National Defence in 1922 and 1923. In 1924, the Royal Canadian Air Force emerged from this organization as a permanent force, remaining in the control of the army until 1938, when it gained full independence.[5]

Canada and the Peacetime Air Training Scheme

A Canadian member of the Royal Air Force, Group Capt. Robert Leckie, DSO, ASC, DFC, was the first to suggest, early in the summer of 1936, the advantages of training schools in Canada. Leckie was in a good position to make a proposal for a Canadian air training plan. During his long career in the Royal Naval Air Service and the Royal Air Force, Leckie had been superintendent of RAF reserves from 1933 to 1936. The Royal Air Force Reserves, commanded by Group Capt. Arthur Tedder (later he became marshal of the RAF, Lord Tedder), formed an important part of the training branch. Leckie drew up a memorandum demonstrating the strategic advantage of Canada as a training centre for the RAF. The memorandum illustrated the closeness of Canada to the United Kingdom and to the United States of America. Another point emphasized in the memorandum was that a training plan on Canadian soil would attract many Canadians to the RAF.[6]

Leckie's idea struck a sympathetic chord with his superiors at the air ministry who remembered the training efforts of Canada during the Great War. In August 1936, Tedder and the British secretary of state for air, Lord Swinton, approached Ian Mackenzie, the Canadian minister of national defence, about the possibility of a scheme for air training in Canada; but, at this early stage, the federal cabinet rejected the proposal, since there was no immediate crisis. The issue of British air training in Canada went dormant again for almost two years.

The question was opened again in May 1938 when the government of the United Kingdom sent a mission, headed by the British industrialist J. G. Weir, to Ottawa to assess the Canadian aircraft industry. When the opportunity arose, Weir was to put forward the air training question. The opportunity came in a meeting between Sir

Frances Floud, the British high commissioner in Ottawa, Weir, and Prime Minister King. King emphasized that he was opposed to British schools being established in Canada. In an account by the prime minister of the meeting, he told the British visitors that Canada "would agree to cooperate to the extent of all the [air training] space they might wish, but that was not what was wanted." King's memorandum also stated the reasons why there could not be any British control. Making a decision that committed Canada to enter any future European war on the side of Britain was seen by King as politically dangerous, with the potential rejection of such a commitment to England by Quebec.[7]

Although King warned the British delegation that disclosing the content of their meeting to the press would do more harm than good, the information appeared in newspapers soon afterwards. This led to criticism by Arthur Meighen, Conservative leader in the Senate, and by R.B. Bennett, the leader of the Opposition in the House of Commons. The attitude of the King government, according to the Opposition, was unacceptable. Political pressure was mounting in many sectors of Canadian society that felt close to Britain and the Empire and wanted Canada's unconditional support of British initiatives. After he had been hard-pressed in the House of Commons, King replied: "We . . . are prepared to have our own establishment here and to give in those establishments facilities [opportunities] to British pilots to come and train here. But they must come and train in establishments which are under the control of the government of Canada and for which the Minister of National Defence will be able to answer in this Parliament with respect to everything concerning them."[8] This ended the issue and became the basis for discussions on the air training question.

Four days later, on July 5, King drafted and sent to the United Kingdom a proposal including an invitation to the British government to send officials to Canada to negotiate an acceptable air training scheme.[9]

Sir Kingsly Wood, the new British secretary of state for air, stated on July 7, in the British House of Commons, that a reply had already been sent "expressing warm appreciation for the offer," and that arrangements had been made "for an officer to be sent immediately to Canada to explore . . . the possibility of working out such a scheme for training facilities in Canada." It was soon found, however, that British expectations were too high and that King's offer had been misinterpreted. King was prepared to discuss the scheme, but was not prepared to commit Canada to train Canadian pilots for Britain. He would have accepted limited numbers of British men to come to Canada to train.[10]

Discussion continued as Britain pressed for a Canadian commitment to train Canadian aircrew for the RAF. Although the negotiations did not achieve such a commitment, the negotiations demonstrated the weakness of Canada's training facilities.

King replied to the proposed air training plan in a letter to the British high commissioner to Canada on September 6, 1938. He stalled the process by asking for more detailed information. This was the end of the issue until December 9 when the British government moved to make the air training plan more acceptable by scaling it down. The new plan called for 135 Canadian pilots without any mention of sending any British recruits.[11]

Prime Minister King's reply of December 31, 1938 again rejected the British proposal, making three points which were essential to Canadian acceptance of the scheme. The first was that only British pilots were to be trained. The second issue was that the numbers were too large. Finally, the schools in Canada must be under the control of the Canadian Department of National Defence.[12]

The negotiations that followed were difficult but an agreement was made two months later. The new plan involved training fifty British candidates for the RAF along with another seventy-five Canadians for the RCAF. This plan was accepted by King because it would train British and not Canadian airmen for the RAF. More important, the plan appeared to be a simple exchange of personnel for air training rather than a commitment to Britain.[13]

The main benefit of the agreement was that it brought a realization of how inadequate the air training facilities were in Canada. Expansion and upgrading of facilities for the eventual British Commonwealth Air Training Plan were already underway. Furthermore, the negotiations that began in July 1938 and continued until April 1939 had brought about an understanding between the RAF and the RCAF on training issues.[14]

The Birth of the British Commonwealth Air Training Plan

On September 10, 1939, the day Canada declared war, there was a meeting at the Air Ministry with Wing Commander H. V. Hickes, the Canadian air liaison officer in London, and RCAF Group Capt. A. F. Godfrey. In the end, it was confirmed that the control over the air training plans would remain with the RCAF.[15]

A message from British Prime Minister Chamberlain to King demonstrated the urgency and importance the British government placed on the Plan. The main point of the message was a call for assistance "to counter German air strength and, in combination with other military measures and economic pressure, to bring ultimate victory."[16] The British called for a minimum of fifty thousand aircrew annually. The closing statement made clear the dramatic need of the training plan:

We hope that you will agree as to the immense influence which the development and realization of such a great project as that outlined in this telegram may have upon the whole course of the war; it might even prove decisive. We trust therefore that this co-operation method of approach to the problem will appeal to your Government. The knowledge that a vast air potential was being built up in the Dominion where no German air activity could interfere with expansion, might well have a psychological effect on the German equal to that produced by the intervention of the United States in the last war with its vast resources.[17]

William Lyon Mackenzie King received the message after dinner on September 26, 1939. The prime minister was impressed with the magnitude and importance that Chamberlain attached to aviation. More important, King observed that, "with concentration of Canadian energies on air training and air power and therefore less pressure for a large army, there would also be less risk of agitation for conscription." The Air Training Plan in Canada as the nation's major contribution to the war effort would minimize the political risks of conscription because the Canadians in the RCAF were to be volunteers.[18]

The proposal came before cabinet on September 28. The result was an agreement in principle and a call for more information and negotiations. This view was outlined in a telegram sent the same day to Chamberlain. King would not allow the RAF to have the same control it had had during the Great War.[19]

The chiefs of staff estimated that Canadian defence would cost $491,689,000 and $150,364,000 would be the cost for air defence. Canada had agreed to give the United Kingdom unlimited credit because of the imbalance of trade that had developed between Britain and the U.S.A., but the costs would be too high with the large expenditures on air training. As a result, the industrialized dominions of the Commonwealth—New Zealand, Australia, and Canada—would have to pay their share. The financing of the Plan became an issue when the leaders of the dominions, who had become conditioned by the Great Depression, did not understand and were unprepared for the massive expenditures of modern warfare. The Canadian cabinet war committee felt it was doing enough. The cost figures put them in a defensive state of mind when the British negotiator, Lord Riversdale, an industrialist and an adviser on the purchase of war materials, arrived in Ottawa on October 14, 1939.[20]

Two days after Riversdale's arrival, a preliminary meeting was held during which the basic proposal was outlined. Almost 29,000 aircrew were to be trained a year. The elementary flying training was to be carried out in the three dominions, then the airmen were to be transferred to Canada for advanced flying training. The entire course of training for air observers, wireless operators, and air gunners was to be carried out in Canada. The Plan proposed twelve elementary flying training schools, twenty-five advanced or service flying training schools, fifteen air observer schools, fifteen bombing and gunnery schools, three air navigation schools, and one large wireless school in Canada. To operate the plan, 54,000 air force personnel and five thousand aircraft would be required.[21]

Air Commodore E. W. Stedman, head of engineering and supply branch of the RAF, was appointed to draw up an estimate of the cost for the Plan for a hypothetical three-year period. His estimate was $989,859,904. After Riversdale adjusted the figures, an estimate of $888.5 million was presented to the members of the Canadian cabinet war committee. This total was further reduced when Riversdale explained that the United Kingdom would supply aircraft, engines, spare parts, and accessories at a value of $140 million. The total then stood at $748.5 million. This total would be split among the three participating countries. Canada was expected to supply half the trainees at half the cost, which would be $374,230,000. Australia and New Zealand were to supply the rest.[22]

Prime Minister King believed Canada's share was far too great. He argued that it was "a scheme suggested by the British government and for which the British must be mainly responsible." King was not alone in his belief. Finance Minister J. L. Ralston agreed that the British contribution had to be higher, otherwise Canada would be bled to death.[23]

The talks became more complicated, including issues of Commonwealth trade. Canada presented two essential conditions for financing the Training Plan. One was that Britain had to buy more Canadian wheat. Second, the amount of Canadian credit given to the United Kingdom had to be restricted. The British government, after deciding that the Air Training Plan was important enough to grant Canada these two conditions, requested that the Plan receive top priority in Canada.[24]

The cost of the Plan was reduced to $607,271,210, with an agreed termination date of March 31, 1943. The United Kingdom would pay $185 million. Canada would pay for initial and elementary flying training at a cost of $66,146,048. The pooled expenditures of the three dominions would be $356,125,162, with 80.64 percent coming from Canada, 11.28 percent from Australia, and 8.08 percent from New Zealand. Canada would pay $287,179,331, Australia $40,170,918, and New Zealand $28,774,913.[25]

The negotiations were completed by the end of November. The selection of air fields was already underway. The British government wanted to proceed immediately with the initialing of the agreement "so that we may . . . take this essential step forward in our joint war effort." Prime Minister King, however, refused to initial the agreement until the earlier Canadian conditions were met, including British purchases of Canadian wheat and the agreement that the Air Training Plan had priority over all other military commitments by Canada. Chamberlain agreed with the trade condition, but was silent on the priority statement. Conscious that a priority statement would help minimize the risks of conscription in Canada, King remained firm, making it clear he wanted a statement suggesting that "participation in the Air Training Scheme would provide more effective assistance than any other form of co-operation which Canada could give."[26]

This was the group of men that negotiated the agreement that brought about the BCATP in December 1939. Front row, left to right: Air Chief Marshal Sir R. Brooke-Popham, RAF; Col. J.L. Ralston, minister of finance, Canada; Group Capt. H. W. L. Saunders, chief of the air staff, New Zealand; Senator R. Dandurand, Canada; Lord Riversdale, United Kingdom; Prime Minister W. L. M. King, Canada; J. V. Fairbairn, minister of air, Australia; E. Lapointe, minister of justice, Canada; Captain H. H. Balfour, undersecretary for air, United Kingdom; N. McL. Rogers, minister of national defence, Canada; Air Marshal Sir C. Courtney, RAF. (PMR 81–152)

After further negotiations, a reply arrived on December 1, 1939: "The United Kingdom Government have informed us that, considering present and future requirements, they feel that participation in the Air Training Scheme would provide for more effective assistance toward our ultimate victory than any other form of cooperation which Canada can give. At the same time they would wish it to be clearly understood that they would welcome no less heartily the presence of Canadian land forces in the theatre of war."[27] Mackenzie King accepted the statement but edited it for his own purpose. The passage used in King's broadcast of December 17 announcing the creation of the Training Plan was: "The United Kingdom Government has informed us that . . . the Plan . . . would provide . . . more effective assistance . . . than any other form of military cooperation which Canada can give. At the same time, the United Kingdom Government wished it to be clearly understood that it would welcome no less heartily the presence of Canadian land forces in the theatre of war *at the earliest possible moment.*"[28] The timing of the announcement and the addition of the last sentiment were very significant. As the broadcast was taking place, Canada's first division was on its way to Britain. The statement suggested that Canada was fulfilling its obligations for land forces at that moment, that the fast arrival of troops rather than large numbers of troops was what mattered the most.[29]

Taking the Plan to the Polls

When Prime Minister King signed the agreement that brought the British Commonwealth Air Training Plan into being, he had won for Canada a role he wanted. With the statement from the United

Kingdom suggesting that Canada's central role was implementing the Air Training Plan and not providing an unlimited supply of land forces, as well as the fact that all aircrew had to be volunteers, King had avoided, for the moment, the divisive issue of conscription.

With the agreement for the Air Training Plan signed, King called an election for March 26, 1940. Canada was now at war, and the nation's role in that war was the central issue of the election. The Opposition called for more commitment to the war effort. The mood of the Canadian public was very different from what it had been during the Great War, when Canadians had little experience of war and no experience in modern wars. They had been certain the war would be over quickly and had wanted every able-bodied man to go overseas to help the Empire win. But the massive losses of that war and the economic stresses it brought had been a shock. No one wanted to experience that again.

King helped his bid for re-election by refusing to announce which communities would receive an air training school, explaining that might be interpreted as interference in the election to the advantage of the Liberal party. With all the schools appearing to be still available, the Liberal party was a logical choice for many voters. With a local member of Parliament who belonged to the Liberal government, there was an increased chance of a community being given a school, along with the accompanying economic development and the opportunity to demonstrate patriotism. Across the Prairies, where the memories of the Great Depression were vivid, the promise of a school and local economic development was too much to ignore.[30]

Mackenzie King easily won the election, capturing 178 of the 245 seats, and he settled into governing Canada through the war years.

2

Preparing for the Great Undertaking

The development of the widely dispersed air training organization expected to consist of 33,000 service personnel and 6,000 civilians demanded a large commitment on the part of the administrators of the Royal Canadian Air Force. At the start of the Second World War, the RCAF had only five aerodromes and six more under construction. For matters of construction, the RCAF had developed a partnership with the Department of Transport during the interwar period. This partnership was extended on October 3, 1939, when Air Vice-Marshal G. M. Croil and J. A. Wilson, the controller of civil aviation, reached an agreement with the department for the rapid expansion of air training facilities. The department was to select sites and, after the approval of the air force, develop landing fields. The air force would design and build the buildings.[1]

Where the Schools Were to Go

The sites for the fields were selected and surveyed even before the agreement for the Air Training Plan was signed. Already, in the summer of 1939, work was underway to expand the existing RCAF schools, which were inadequate even for the prewar training work of the RCAF. The pace of construction accelerated as soon as the formal agreement that brought about the British Commonwealth Air Training Plan was signed.[2]

A major reorganization of the RCAF was needed to administer the new facilities. It was soon obvious that the responsibilities of the RCAF and the Air Training Plan were too large for the Department of National Defence to administer. The three services of the navy, army, and air force had to be separated with expanded administrations. K. S. Maclachan held the post of acting associate deputy minister for the navy and air from September 8, 1939, until April 11, 1940, when James S. Duncan, who had been the senior executive of Massey Harris Company Ltd., was appointed associate acting deputy minister for air.

At the same time, German successes in Denmark and Norway in the spring of 1940 made it obvious to cabinet that even more expansion of Canadian military forces was required. The result was the creation of new ministries for the air force and the navy. The former postmaster general, C. G. ("Chubby") Power, was appointed minister of national defence for air on May 23, 1940. In July, a similar ministry was created for the navy.[3]

Private Business and the New Air Schools

Civil aviation played an important role in the Air Training Plan. The Canadian Flying Clubs Association obtained the role of administrating elementary flying training schools for its member clubs. The role of administrating the elementary schools was not unexpected because eight of the flying clubs had been training pilots for the RCAF in cities across Canada since June, 1939. As well, fourteen more clubs obtained contracts at the outbreak of the war. The clubs had to prove that they had the resources to provide adequate instructional, administrative, and technical staff for each proposed school. Once the clubs demonstrated their financial stability and technical ability, they were given a contract reorganizing them into Crown corporations known as flying training companies. The contracts allowed for monthly managerial fees, an allowance for operation and maintenance, a set payment per flying hour, and a ration allowance. Major equipment such as aircraft was supplied by the government. These payments, which allowed for a five percent profit, were subject to periodic revision. Any balance over five percent profit was placed in a government-controlled fund. By organizing the elementary flying schools this way, the government was able to make use of qualified civilian pilots, as instructors, and existing facilities for the war effort. This saved both money and time in the establishment of the Plan.[4]

Establishing Air Observer Schools

The air observer schools, which gave instruction in flight navigation, were administered by larger commercial aviation companies. Often the same facilities used for elementary flying schools were also home to observer schools until 1942, when the Air Training Plan was reorganized and many of the air observer schools were expanded and separated from the elementary flying schools.

The contracts for the air observer schools closely resembled the agreements that established the elementary flying training schools, with one notable difference. The agreements establishing the air observer schools did not make allowances for a five percent profit to the operating companies. The payments to the operating

In May 1940, the men were hard at work in the drafting room of the Directorate of Works and Buildings as they prepared blueprints for the air training schools. (PMR 79–133)

companies were adjusted to cover only the actual costs of the training. All the air observer training was provided by air force personnel. Civilian pilots were provided by the companies to fly the students and their instructors on their exercises. The civilian pilots, who were often called "taxi drivers" or "air chauffeurs," guided student navigators when they directed the pilot off course during navigational exercises.[5]

The flying schools in the West featured a wide variety of aircraft. Whatever was available was used. The two most common aircraft at the elementary flying schools on the Prairies were the Tiger Moth, and, later, the Fairchild Cornell. Early in the war, a number of Fleet Finches were also in service for training. Another uncommon type of aircraft, the Fort Fleet, was used at the wireless school in Calgary. At the service flying schools, the bombing and gunnery schools, and the air observer schools, the most widely used aircraft were the double-engined Avro Ansons and Cessna Cranes. Other common aircraft also at these kinds of schools were Harvards, Hurricanes, Fairey Battles, Bristol Bolingbrokes, and Westland Lysanders, just to name a few. The RAF service flying training schools had Airspeed Oxfords as well.

Schools opened, closed, and were transferred throughout the war. Elementary

A Lockheed 10A Electra CF-BAF aircraft used by Canadian Airways Limited. Canadian Airways was one of the largest airlines in western Canada before the war and won the contract to operate an air observer school. (JRA 015304821)

flying training schools were located at Lethbridge, High River, Assiniboia, De Winton, Bowden, Caron, Pearce, Portage la Prairie, Virden, Davidson, Yorkton, and Neepawa. Service flying training schools were established in Macleod, Weyburn, Claresholm, Vulcan, Moose Jaw, Medicine Hat, Penhold, Estevan, Swift Current, Dauphin, Yorkton, Brandon, North Battleford, Souris, Gimli, and Carberry. Larger centres such as Winnipeg received more than one school; that city had a wireless school and an air observer school. Regina and Edmonton each received an initial training school, an elementary flying school, and air observer school. Saskatoon received an initial training school and a service flying training school. Calgary received a service flying school and a wireless school. Prince Albert had both an elementary flying school and an air observer school. The community of Portage la Prairie was the host of an air observer school, while Rivers received the central navigation school. Bombing and gunnery schools, which needed to be more isolated, were constructed at Mossbank, Lethbridge, MacDonald, Dafoe, and Paulson. A flying instructor school was established at Vulcan, then transferred in 1943 to Pearce, Alberta.

Residents of Yorkton inspect the new air buildings and runways on the opening day of the service flying training school. There was no disappointment as western Canadians saw what they had achieved on their opening days. (RA 7109[1])

The Royal Air Force Schools

Not all the air training schools in the BCATP were administered by Royal Canadian Air Force personnel. A number of schools were run by the Royal Air Force. During the negotiations that led to the Plan, the British government suggested that at some point during the war it might prove necessary to transfer service schools from Britain to Canada. Nothing more was said about this idea until the war worsened for the Allied cause in the spring of 1940. With the fall of Norway, Denmark, and France, all British airfields and airspace were needed for operations, and air training activities could no longer be sustained in Britain. The Canadian government was informed that the United Kingdom wished to transfer four RAF service flying training schools to Canada.[6]

Canada responded positively to this request after it was agreed that the costs for the schools would be covered by the British government. With Canadian acceptance, the RAF revised the request to include eight service flying training schools, two air observer schools, one bombing and gunnery school, one air navigation school, one general reconnaissance school, and one torpedo bombing school. While facilities were being established, the RAF personnel arrived to begin training in partly completed schools. In March 1941, the burden was increased again when the RAF requested an additional nine service flying training schools, fifteen elementary flying training schools, ten air observer schools, and four operational training units. Again, Canada accepted these schools because Britain was

American, New Zealand, and British airmen line up at clothing stores to receive new kits. The cooperation between the aircrew of all nationalities was obvious throughout the Air Training Plan. (PL 5288)

paying for them. With these new developments, many more facilities had to be established. The prairie provinces received the largest number of new schools: Alberta received six, Saskatchewan eight, and Manitoba two RAF schools.[7] The RAF elementary flying training schools in the Prairies were located at Neepawa, Caron, Assiniboia, Moose Jaw, Estevan, Swift Current, De Winton, Bowden, Pearce, Medicine Hat, Penhold, and Calgary; the service schools of the RAF at Carberry, Weyburn, and North Battleford.

The legal status of the British schools in Canada was defined by the Visiting Forces Acts of Canada and Britain. In 1933, both countries had passed acts allowing the easy transfer of service personnel from one country to the next. When the RAF schools were established in Canada, they were declared by the governments as "acting in combination," meaning that they mutually agreed to work together. As long as the RAF personnel were in Canada, they were to follow RCAF administrative and operational control. The RAF were given access to supplies and the medical services of the RCAF. The RCAF also supplied maintenance facilities to the RAF schools. The British fully cooperated with the RCAF while they were in Canada, although each service kept its national identity and personnel were commanded by their own officers. The air personnel were also allowed to follow their own customs and traditions. The RAF followed its own routines and rules, which differed very little from those of the RCAF.[8]

Training for All the Allies

The Air Training Plan was established to train the majority of the aircrew for the Allies during the war. As a result, trainees arrived from Australia, New Zealand, India, and other countries of the Commonwealth. Aircrew of other nationalities who had joined the Allies after the fall of their countries were also trained, but the numbers of trainees from countries not in the Commonwealth remained small with nearly 2,000 Free French, about 900 Czechoslovakians, 677 Norwegians, 450 Poles, and about the same number of Belgians and Dutch receiving training. However, the majority of the trainees were British and Canadian and the proportion of trainees from other countries was small.[9]

3

Building for the Future

The coming of the Air Training Plan was dramatic for the Prairies, which was just emerging from nearly a decade of Depression, as it promised millions of dollars of development. With the two unrelated phenomena of the worldwide economic depression and a prolonged drought, the Prairies had suffered more than any other region in Canada during the 1930s. For other regions, the worst of the Depression was over by mid-1933, but in Manitoba, Saskatchewan, and Alberta, the worst years were 1936 and 1937. There was a great expectation across the West that the region would benefit substantially from the Air Training Plan.[1]

Communities that hoped to win a school had to demonstrate the ability to provide services it would need: roads, sewers, electric power, and water. Communities or sites in mountainous regions, with their safety hazards, or within five miles of the United States border, over which student pilots might stray, were not considered. The bombing and gunnery schools needed very large areas, about one hundred square miles, in order to avoid any danger to people or property. The navigation schools required regions to fly over containing as many different types of geography as possible, including bodies of water.

When a site fulfilled the requirements, its value as a postwar civil or military airport was considered, with locations appearing to have potential as an active airport after the war preferred.

The value of each site was considered in terms of what it would contribute to the training command it was associated with. Every command was to have all elements of aircrew training available, as well as all of the services needed to sustain the training effort. Each of the four training commands was to be self-sufficient, with its own recruiting organization, supply depots, repair depots, and training schools. In all four commands, there were initial schools, elementary flying schools, service flying schools, air observer schools, bombing and gunnery schools, and wireless schools. Sites that contributed to any one of the training commands were given preference.[2]

Lobbying for Schools

Most of the large cities across the Prairies had no fear that they would be ignored in the Air Training Plan. Winnipeg, Prince Albert, Regina, Saskatoon, and Calgary had been given notification of the establishment of air training facilities as early as the January before the federal election of March, 1940. The cities were obvious choices as they each had a large population and the services needed and could benefit from the establishment of an airport or an upgraded airport.

By the autumn of 1940, the city of Edmonton realized the assumption that the city would automatically receive one of the largest facilities because of its existing airport was a mistake. The *Edmonton Journal* reported that lobbying would be needed because the city had only received an air observer school: "Announcement of the airport development expansion came within a few hours after the Edmonton chamber of commerce had protested to Ottawa that the plans for the airport were meagre in comparison with those for other centres." The newspaper printed the contents of the protest that had been sent to Ottawa: "Edmonton businessmen are becoming disappointed over the meagre plans for the development of Edmonton's airport compared with what is being done at other points in Alberta, such as Calgary, Macleod, Medicine Hat, and Penhold, which cannot be regarded as more important than Edmonton in this respect. . . . The city has made strong representations which have been supported by this chamber of commerce that Edmonton insists on being equitably dealt with in this matter."[3]

The call for more participation in Edmonton was answered when the city became the host of the Number Sixteen Elementary Flying Training School on November 11, 1940 and was given Number Four Initial Training School in the summer of 1941.

Students gather around a map at the photographic section at air observer school in Edmonton. The air observer school was established at Edmonton before the elementary school. (JRA 01534807)

Call for Their Share

Edmonton was not the only community to complain about not receiving its share when the first schools were announced. Don O'Hearn, an airframe mechanic, recalled that "There was a lot of lobbying by politicians and would-be politicians to get a base in his town, to get a plant nearby. A lot of them were lobbying to get an airfield because of the construction jobs it would bring, but there would also be a lot of military people there that would spend money in the community."[4] A large number of communities across the Prairies that were angered by their absence from the first list, which included only the larger cities in the West, began lobbying efforts. The larger centres that received major facilities—Estevan, North Battleford, Yorkton, and Moose Jaw—had all followed the same pattern of lobbying for these establishments. These towns and cities acted by passing resolutions in their councils requesting that their area be considered for future air training facilities. These requests were then carried to Ottawa by civic delegations. Local members of Parliament pursued the same goals. The mayor of Moose Jaw even wrote directly to the minister of national defence to win a facility for his city. The decision to locate a school at Moose Jaw had already been made but had not been announced.[5]

Two communities that had unsuccessful campaigns to win an air training school were Rosetown and Melville. Both felt they had a "just claim" for a facility in their communities because they felt that their location was equal to others that had received schools. Civic delegations passed resolutions calling on the federal government to place airports in their communities, then carried them to Ottawa. However, these towns did not stop there. Both took steps to locate more wells for a better guarantee of an adequate water supply and pledged to supply roads, sewers, and power if schools were located at their centres.[6]

Melville made a strong claim based on the fact that it was a railway centre with buildings, shops, and tradesmen available because of the CNR and the town's poor economic condition since the railroad left the community. In the summer of 1940, Melville claimed:

The Melville and District Board of Trade has no wish to embarrass the Government with extravagant demands on behalf of this community, but believing that it has an obligation to the town, has petitioned the authorities regarding the "just" claims in connection with war developments. The board has pointed out that the town of Melville was developed as a railroad town and on the understanding that it would continue as a divisional point. The town has been one of the hardest hit by unemployment since the Canadian National Railways moved the superintendent's office staff to Saskatoon in 1934 and the car shops closed as well as other railway work curtailed. At peak, over 200 families were in receipt of relief in this town of 4,000 population. The car shops were reopened two years ago, though not to former capacity, and increased railway traffic lately has improved . . . but there are still 100 families on relief. In view of these facts, the trade board believes that Melville should receive every consideration when the Government is allotting new airports etc. because the present unfavourable position of the towns is due primarily to the previous action of the nationally owned railway.[7]

This somewhat emotional appeal for an air training school did not result in a positive reply. No reasons were given for denying any community a school.

Placing the Schools

A pattern in the allocation of schools across the Prairies was emerging. Most Liberal constituencies received a school early in the war, followed by constituencies that had a CCF member of Parliament, especially those CCF constituencies that had previously been Liberal. Melville was an exception to the pattern because it had been a longtime supporter of the Liberal party and continued to elect Liberals during and after the war. Few Conservative constituencies received facilities.

The chances of receiving an air training school appeared to be reduced in towns that had a railway depot. It was clear from the comments in the *Souris Plaindealer* that general disappointment prevailed in communities that were passed over when the first schools were announced. The newspaper reported that Sir Edward Beatty, president of the Canadian Pacific Railway, had given his annual address to the CPR luncheon club at Montreal, and drew "sharp attention to the fact that 'special advantages' have been given to the nationally-owned railway in the location of war industries." He went on to state that:

It has been most unfortunate that, owing to the possession by the state of a railway system which has involved the public treasury in colossal losses, there has been a very real pressure on the government to make some effort to give the publicly-owned railway an advantage over this company in connection with the development of war industries. It has been the duty of the management of this company to impress on the government that those Canadian citizens who are in the employ of the Canadian Pacific Railways are as much entitled to share in the stimulated business activities of the nation as are workers of the competing system.

The Plaindealer editorialized that Beatty's point was well taken.

At a Souris Board of Trade committee meeting a few weeks ago, The Plaindealer *drew the attention of the members to the fact that up to the present every air school established in Manitoba has been located on the Canadian National Railway. As Sir Edward Beatty says, the railway employees of the Canadian Pacific have an equal right to share in the stimulated business created by these activities of the nation.*

This policy of the government is not only unfair to Canadian Pacific employees; it is having the effect of bringing towns like Souris to a state of unnecessary stagnation through citizens having to abandon their homes and move to CNR towns in order to get war employment.[8]

There was no evidence to support the claim that CNR towns received more air training facilities than CPR towns, however. In fact, Souris was given Number 17 Service Flying Training School in March, 1943, after this report appeared in the *Souris Plaindealer*.

Newspapers across Saskatchewan reported much wider political lobbying in that province than did newspapers in Alberta and Manitoba. Considering that when the first schools were established in 1940, Saskatchewan had eleven, Alberta six, and Manitoba two, lobbying appears to have had some effect. As more schools were needed, Saskatchewan became host to approximately 40 percent of those in the Prairies, while Alberta claimed about 33 percent, and Manitoba won 26 percent.

4

For Duty and Prosperity

In all the communities given air training facilities, the reaction was very positive. Residents looked forward to the prosperity expected to result from the establishment of the schools. Although economic development was important, the opportunity to help with the war effort by contributing to the Air Training Plan was central. Indeed, Phil Ellison, an air gunner trained in the Plan, remembered that "The general feeling was that we had to get the people trained and this war won."[1] However, the communities also wanted to build for the future.

In Rivers, Manitoba, *The Gazette* demonstrated the importance of the Plan to the West when it told its readers:

> *Thirty-three years ago, when the Grand Trunk Pacific was pushed west across the prairies, the mushroom town that sprung up in Manitoba was Rivers. . . . So rapid was its growth, comments Graham Barker in the Winnipeg Free Press, that housing accommodations were unavailable. Tents were hastily thrown up, shacks appeared almost overnight. Then came a change. Railroad equipment, men and materials were transferred to other points, homes were vacated. In time, the houses began to tumble down, others were destroyed by fire. Rivers, finally, had just comfortable living rooms for "those present."*
>
> *Then came decisions to turn the local Trans-Canada Air Lines landing field into an air training school. For a couple of years back the personnel of Rivers airfield lived in cottages erected on the field. But a few months ago, contracts with their equipment besieged that station. The one small hotel, every home and block and suite within Rivers was visited with a view of obtaining room. Tents again were thrown up, the workers sought out farm homes. And every freight train brought more men and more material. Stores and other places of business were experiencing, night and day, a swift exchange of goods such as has not been seen since the day of the railroad expansion. For the second time in its short existence Rivers is seeing boom times.*[2]

Larger communities, such as Edmonton, Regina, and Winnipeg, had local contractors to construct the airport facilities. In smaller centres, such as Macleod, Brandon, Vulcan, and Virden, contractors were brought in to do the construction work. Local contractors in these smaller centres found that they were occupied with subcontracts to construct small buildings, supply materials, and lay gravel and to do other necessary work.[3]

It was clear that there was enough work for everyone when the Lethbridge *Herald* reported on construction work in Alberta during 1940:

> *Large numbers of skilled tradesmen and laborers are employed at different points in south Alberta where contractors are busy preparing different units of the Commonwealth Air Training Plan.*
>
> *At Macleod, Bennett and White Construction Co. has started the big job of*

erecting buildings to accommodate the service flying school to be established there. Buildings at this site will cover several acres and a large gang of workmen is employed.

At the same point approximately half a mile south of Macleod, Fred Manning and Co. are carrying out a large contract for constructing runways. Thousands of yards of dirt are being moved. The same contractor is grading a landing area three miles north of Pearce.

Half way between Macleod and Granum and three miles east of the highway, Dutton Bros. of Calgary are grading a large landing area and constructing hard-surfaced runways. These three airports are all part of the Macleod training school.

Work on the Medicine Hat Service Flying school is also being rushed. General Construction Co. of Vancouver is grading the Medicine Hat airport and constructing hard-surfaced runways. The same contractor is constructing hard-surfaced runways at Holsom airport, west of Medicine Hat. D. Smith of Maple Creek is speeding the job of grading the landing area at the airport north of Whitla.[4]

The provincial highway agencies did the majority of the contour work for the airport sites. Provincial health departments cooperated in the analysis of water supplies. Some municipalities acted before the allocation of the schools to find adequate water supplies while others searched for water during the construction of the schools.

The work of the host communities in support of nearby schools, however, went far beyond supplying water. Saskatoon City Council reported the construction and maintenance of water and sewage mains to the airport. Virden and Wynyard reported they were required to supply extra electrical power to the air training stations located nearby. Lethbridge constructed and maintained oiled gravel roads. Services that were requested and delivered also included fire protection in Davidson and ambulance services in Saskatoon. In all cases, municipal and city councils made the necessary expenditures for the local schools.

Worthwhile Investment for the Future

Although the provincial and municipal governments were required to pay the costs for services to the local schools, the investment appeared to be worth the expense. The local economies grew. From the earliest announcement of the location of a school near a community, the economic benefits were heralded in the press. Typical of the

The original instructors of the elementary flying school at Lethbridge in 1940. From left to right: Joe Patton, Homer Thompson, Bill Roy, Jock Palmer, Bill Smith, Ken Piper, Frank Hawthorne, Fred Lasby. (NA–3277–25)

Air training facilities were needed urgently and construction, like this scene from Yorkton, continued regardless of mud and any other difficulties that might arise. (RA 7098[1])

reports found in local newspapers about the construction of the airport facilities and what it meant to the local economy was the article, "700 Men on the Job Within Three Weeks," printed in *The Estevan Mercury*:

Construction of the building at Estevan's Service Flying Training School will commence within the next week. The Mercury was told on Thursday by W. J. Greenfield, general superintendent of the Bird Construction Co. of Winnipeg and Regina, the firm which has the contract. Total costs of the buildings will be about $1,000,000, Mr. Greenfield said. This added to the figures previously quoted for the construction of the runways indicates the total expenditure for the School will be between $1,775,000 and $2,000,000.

As soon as the ground is staked on the north east quarter of the main field opposite to the Koch farm four miles south of Estevan, construction of the buildings will be underway, Mr. Greenfield said.

Peak employment of 500 men will be reached within three weeks, he stated, and his company's monthly payroll would be in the neighborhood of $50,000.

Carter-Halls-Aldinger, the firm holding the contract for building the runways, expects to have more than 200 men on the job within the next two weeks."[5]

These reports were common in those communities that participated in the Air Training Plan. No urban centre was too large to note the benefits gained by construction at its airport.

During construction of the air stations, some towns took advantage of the heavy equipment around to do work that would otherwise be too expensive. When equip-

Mossbank was a typical bombing and gunnery school with the runways built in a triangle, allowing for changes of wind direction. (PL 1679)

ment arrived to do the asphalt work at the airfields in Weyburn, the city engineer reported he was considering using the equipment to asphalt "several blocks in the downtown business-section of the city, the finishing to be done by the company that is now carrying out similar work at Weyburn airport. . . ." In the enthusiasm of the moment, Weyburn also used the opportunity to install name plates for all the streets for the first time.[6]

Hope for the Future

Communities that had benefited from the construction of air training facilities were positive about the reduction of people in need of relief. They also looked forward to what the new airport would bring after the war. This sentiment was revealed in the Lethbridge *Herald* when it reported that Robert Wilkinson, manager of the local air training school, said he believed Lethbridge would become "one of the great flying centres of America, especially when the 'inside route' from Mexico to Alaska is built."[7]

In 1943, the Rivers *Gazette* pointed out:

The rapid development in aviation since the beginning of the war has awakened the interest of people everywhere in the post-war possibilities for the use of the airplane. As the planes for the air routes of the future are discussed it becomes increasingly apparent that Canadians have yet another national asset in the skies above us. Early in the war it was found that the shortest air route between this continent and Britain was via Canada and as a result the RAF

Ferry Command now known as the RAF Transport Command, established headquarters in the East. From an unknown point large numbers of airplanes, manufactured in Canada and the United States, are flown to Britain with great success. A beginning has been made in transport freight over this route and there is little doubt but that passenger and freight traffic will continue to use the skies after the war.[8]

The gains made during the war in these communities would be held onto as protection against any future economic difficulties.

One flying instructor, Jim Kirk, remembered that "even little towns and hamlets were involved, especially if there was an air force station around, because there were shops. Even farmers were supplying fresh eggs, milk and all that kind of thing. All the places in town, like bowling alleys, stores, civilians selling clothes, even what would be expensive clothes; men would buy them just to go on leave. Prosperity was evident everywhere. . . . Some of the fellows on some of the stations even had their own cars."[9]

The wealth that the Plan brought went beyond the economic gain the community received. The towns and cities felt closer to the war effort because of the existence of local BCATP schools. When the school closed at Swift Current in March 1944, *The Sun* reported: "The government put a lot of money into the buildings and equipment here, but in terms of victory and a return to normal living again under the banner of Peace, it will have been money well spent, even if they have to scrap the 'whole darn shooting match' for junk. The men who trained here shot down Messerschmidts and dropped explosive eggs on war factories in Berlin. That all helped to hasten the day when our lads will be coming home again."[10]

5

"Cheered in the Streets"

After the air training schools had been built, the next step was the coming of the air force personnel and the air trainees. Both the arrival of these men and the opening ceremonies at the schools were significant events in the host communities. These events were well planned to show a warm welcome. The *Weyburn Review* reported the arrival of seventy-five British on Christmas Day, 1941:

> *A hundred or more people headed by Mayor J. K. Brimacombe and J. H. Warren chairmen of the Weyburn War Auxiliary Services committee waited at the station for the train which was an hour and a half late to arrive. The airmen following roll call on the station platform were whisked in private cars to the Canadian Legion hall where they were warmly welcomed and served with steaming hot coffee, sandwiches and doughnuts, with Canadian Legion Ladies Auxiliary members doing honors in the kitchen while Legionnaires served the newcomers and others who had assembled in the dining room of the hall. The hot coffee and lunch were greatly appreciated by the airmen who had spent many hours on the train trip to Weyburn.*[1]

One airman remembered the sentiment that came with the Air Training Plan when he wrote, "We were told we were great and we began to believe it. We really weren't any different, of course, but we had some self confidence which had been almost lost in the decade before the war during the Great Depression. Men who had to stand like beggars in bread lines in those years were cheered in the streets."[2]

The Prairies at Last

Upon their arrival, airmen of all nationalities found themselves in a very different environment and culture. The Swift Current *Sun* reported that when the British airmen arrived in June, one commented, "This sure is a cold country," but then a local resident replied, "Just wait till you've been here a winter."

The *Moose Jaw Times-Herald* commented in November, 1940: "There was a strange medley of clothing among the men, for some were dressed to meet the sub-zero weather that faced them in Moose Jaw while others were wearing summer 'shorts' and no underwear, though the latter had been issued to them and was packed away for the trip to Western Canada."[3]

The *North Battleford News* reported a typical welcome of, "a large crowd of enthusiastic citizens, who were entertained by the City Band." Added to this was an "Indian Welcome," that was led by "the head chief of the Battle River Cree [who] extended a greeting as old as their tribal story to 'the Thunder Birds of Great White Chiefs.'" The chief had "journeyed many miles on foot under a blistering sun to be on hand when the personnel of the Royal Air Force arrived from Great Britain at No. 35 S.F.T.S. here. Chief Swimmer, whose band perpetuates the glorious memory of 'Sweet Grass' the treaty haymaker, donned his ceremonial dress in honor of the arrival of the King's 'braves.' He passed through the ranks of the newly arrived R.A.F. personnel, welcoming each in turn to the land of his forefathers. With him, also in tribute dress, was George Poplar, a councillor of the Sweetgrass band."[4]

What Have We Got Ourselves Into?

In the station publication at Moose Jaw, *The Prairie Flyer*, Corporal T. S. M. Guard admitted, "Many of us have come to dislike the Prairies because we find them dull and uninteresting. It is a bitter sight for us to travel by train, the land is like a vast pancake as we speed across it, and it is especially drab in winter when it is brown and white with no trees to break the monotony."[5]

Robert Steel was one British member of the advanced party to arrive in Moose Jaw in "tropical gear" on October 26, 1940. They were picked up by trucks "which headed out on the open highway, on the wrong side of the road until we reached a group of buildings under construction in the middle of a field full of mud. Welcome home!" The next morning, the group received "real eggs and bacon, the inevitable porridge, toast, and coffee. As a bonus, each person was given a *free* Toronto *Globe and Mail* where we read that we were all 'heroes of the Battle of Britain' and that somewhere in our

A crowd examines aircraft at opening of Dauphin service flying training school. The importance of the school to the local residents is clear in the enthusiasm they show at this opening-day ceremony. (FPA 128138356)

The RCAF band and new recruits parade east on Portage Avenue between Fort and Garry streets in Winnipeg. The air force bands were prominent in many communities that were host to an air school. (FPA 128138362)

The Yorkton air training school opens with the fanfare of a flying show for local residents. The new asphalt runways and the aircraft impressed the people at the warm summer day's events. (RA 7110[1])

A large crowd gathers at the elementary flying training school at High River, Alberta, for a flying demonstration. (NA–4943–2)

midst was 'the lost man of Dunkerque." Steel remembered that: "On complaining to the workmen, who were feverishly working to finish more buildings, about the weather, we were told, 'If you think this is bad, wait till summer comes', and that became the stock answer to anybody who complained about anything."[6]

In one case, a noncommissioned officer from Ontario wrote a letter to his aunt which was published in the *Picton Times*: "Here I am away out in the muddy West typing you a letter when I should be in Cherry Valley spearing pike. . . . This is a barren little town of about 5,000 people but the people are OK, nearly everyone has been out for dinner or supper at some time and they converted their town hall into the loveliest hostess club you ever saw." Blackouts were complete in Britain from the beginning of the war, but this was not the case in Canada. One British airman, upon his arrival in Moose Jaw stated, "Blimey! Look at the lights."[7]

Opening Ceremonies

In most cases, the opening ceremonies included an open house where civilians of the host communities were shown the station's operations, the day ending with a dance. The Saskatoon *Star Phoenix* presented an opening day of an air training school: "People of Saskatoon and district trekked and rode by the thousands along the No. 12 highway from early afternoon and streamed over the airport area viewing the working of the school in actual operation. . . . After the short opening ceremonies, six of the fast, single-engine Harvard training planes and six of the big twin-engine Avro Ansons gave a demonstration of the aerobatics and formation flying, part of the daily training routine."[8]

Other opening ceremonies had different activities. In Prince Albert, there was an address by Prime Minister Mackenzie King. In Yorkton, a baseball game was held on the opening day.

6

Going Through the Mill

Training high numbers of quality aircrew was the central goal of the BCATP. The result was a training program that was unforgiving to those candidates who did not quickly grasp the lessons they were taught. The high stresses of training and the added difficulties for many from other countries around the world of adjusting to a harsh climate and learning a new language was overcome only by determination, discipline, and enthusiasm. It was these attributes among those in the Training Plan that led to its success.

For many of the recruits, both the armed services and air training was new. For the small numbers of Free French, Indian, Czechoslovakian, Norwegian, Polish, Belgian, and Dutch, there was the problem of not knowing English. There were even pilot candidates who, because of the Depression, never had an opportunity to learn to drive a car. Many recruits had not even travelled much beyond their home towns before they entered training. The experience of training began when the volunteers arrived in the recruitment offices where all the essential forms were filled out and signed.

Wet Pea

In the first two years the Plan was in operation, volunteers had to have junior matriculation, which was grade twelve in British Columbia and Ontario and grade eleven in the other provinces. Those who did not have this level of education were told to go back to school. This changed in October 1941, when the number of qualified recruits declined significantly. The RCAF implemented an aptitude test designed to measure the abilities of the trainees who did not meet the academic requirements. Those who scored well on the test were sent to the War Emergency Training Program (known to many airmen as the *Wet Pea*) to upgrade their personal skills. Twenty-seven hundred aircrew received this kind of upgrading.[1]

Bill Minor remembered what that Wartime Emergency Training Plan in Calgary was like: "This [training] consisted mainly of mathematics, aircraft recognition, a little bit of wireless. They speeded us up on our math and they didn't accept 50 or 60 per cent, they wanted it to be 100 per cent on simple mathematics and speed." Minor recalled that he "lived out" in Calgary: "They paid us thirty-seven dollars a month for living out, while we took this training at Central High School downtown. I was lucky to get a place for thirty dollars a month. We didn't have to be in barracks, we were doing what we pleased, but we had to be in class at nine o'clock in the morning."[2]

Manning Depot

Volunteers who had either met the academic standards or had completed War Time Emergency Training were sent to the manning pools, holding facilities where the

Kitchen staff join the men for this photo of a typical airmen's mess. (JRA 015204801)

LAC Rajinder Singh Sandhu, from India, prepares for a training flight, with his parachute secured. For many of the local residents of Weyburn, the war was the first time they had ever seen Sikhs in their traditional turbans. (PL 23202)

trainees received an initial introduction to service life. The experience was often surprising. One airman, C. A. (Smokey) Robson, remembered that his first sight of the depot was from the back of the truck that was bringing the new recruits to the train station: "The grounds were full of people, who were already there, out doing drills. As our truck was driving up the street to the buildings, they all stopped and in a uniform voice yelled *suckers*!"[3]

Another recruit, who became a flying instructor, Stan Morris, recalled: "After the first day of marching, I think if I had been a little closer to home, I would have gone there. My feet were sore. It was a real experience."[4] Phil Ellison, an airgunner, wondered "what the emphasis on marching, squad drilling and banging your feet to the ground had to do with winning a war."[5] The shocks and difficulties were all taken in stride as the civilian recruits became air personnel.

After an interview with an officer, a decision was made as to where a recruit would be sent for training. Bill Minor recalled his experience of being tested and interviewed at the manning depot: "I had an interview with an officer who said I would make a very good wireless air gunner, but my brother was a gunner, and he told me, never go to wireless air gunner; if you want to be a gunner, be a gunner. So, I was a little stubborn. The thing was, they needed wireless air gunners and it had nothing to do with my aptitude test, so I stuck to my guns. Finally he said, alright, we'll send you to [an initial training school], but I don't think you'll ever make a pilot. You know, all they were doing was brain washing kids, that's all."[6]

As historian Fred Hatch pointed out in

RCAF recruits file applications at a recruiting station. Statistics show that the men and women in the Prairies had the highest rate of enlistment in the air force on a per capita basis when compared to the other regions of Canada. (FPA 128138361)

his book, *The Aerodrome of Democracy*, the selection for the pilots was based on fitness and learning ability. The pilot trainees had to undergo three major medical examinations. The first was completed at the recruitment offices, another occurred at the manning depot, and the final and most probing examination was carried out at the initial school. The final medical exam checked for the smallest variation in blood pressure, vision, or heart action. The pilot candidate could have a maximum height of six feet three inches and a maximum weight of two hundred pounds. He had to have passed his eighteenth birthday, but not be over twenty-eight. As manpower shortages developed, the age requirements dropped to seventeen and increased to thirty-five.[7]

Pilot candidates were sent to initial flying training schools, while recruits who demonstrated a high level of mechanical ability were sent to St. Thomas, Ontario, where they learned aircraft body design, engine maintenance, or instrument repairs. Trainees selected for gunnery attended bombing and gunnery schools and navigator candidates were sent to air observer schools located at Edmonton, Regina, Winnipeg, Prince Albert, and Portage la Prairie. Other recruits trained at wireless schools, located at Winnipeg and Calgary, where they learned radio, electronics, and communications.

Initial Training School

At initial training school, candidates were expected to follow a strict routine of classes, marching, cleaning, and physical training. There was no flying training at initial schools. It was a ground school where trainees learned the basics of aeronautics and mathematics. One airman who became an air gunner, Phil Ellison, remembered that the courses taught at the initial school often presented a challenge to the candidate: "I was out of school for three years—to go back to the trigonometry and mathematics that was involved in ground training you had to do some studying. Everybody did work hard. The guys were not fooling around, they were trying hard. They were going to be 'Battle of Britain Aces' if they could get pilot training."[8]

Because many candidates who were sent to the initial training schools were more suited to other trades, the instructors had to determine the aptitudes of the trainees and recommend what type of school they should be sent to next. After completing training at the initial school, the candidates were interviewed by a board. The interviews were the last step in determining who would be selected for pilot training at the elementary flying school. If there was any reason to doubt a candidate's ability to be a pilot, he was selected for one of the other trades such as navigation, wireless, or gunnery and sent to one of the schools that taught that trade.

At Last, Flight!

At the elementary flying training schools, the pilots in training were finally allowed to fly single engine aircraft. They had to learn all the basics of flight, navigation, and gunnery. The course was about eight weeks long, including approximately 50 hours of flying and 126 hours of ground lectures. Later in the war, when the need for pilots was reduced, the flying time was increased to sixty hours with a maximum of seventy-five hours for those who needed it. A pilot trainee was expected to take his first solo flight after eight hours of dual flight. The solo flight was a problem for many. If a candidate was not able to fly solo when expected, he was tested by the chief flying instructor. Most were reassigned to a different air trade.

The syllabus for elementary school was very demanding. Students were expected to progress quickly. Only those who were determined to make their first solo and execute spin recoveries, nearly perfect

Recruits gather at a typical RCAF centre. (PL 20912)

This cockpit drill trainer is being used at Medicine Hat's service flying training school in December 1943. The drill cockpit was a safe place for student pilots to learn the basics of flight. (PMR 81–138)

At the wireless school at Calgary trainees learn flag signalling. Other skills the airmen needed were radio operations and Morse code. (PL 1520)

Three students, E. M. Romilly, RCAF; W. H. Betts, RAAF; and J. A. Mahoud, RAF, train to be observers in an Avro Anson at the air navigation school near Rivers, Manitoba, on June 4, 1941. (PL 3740)

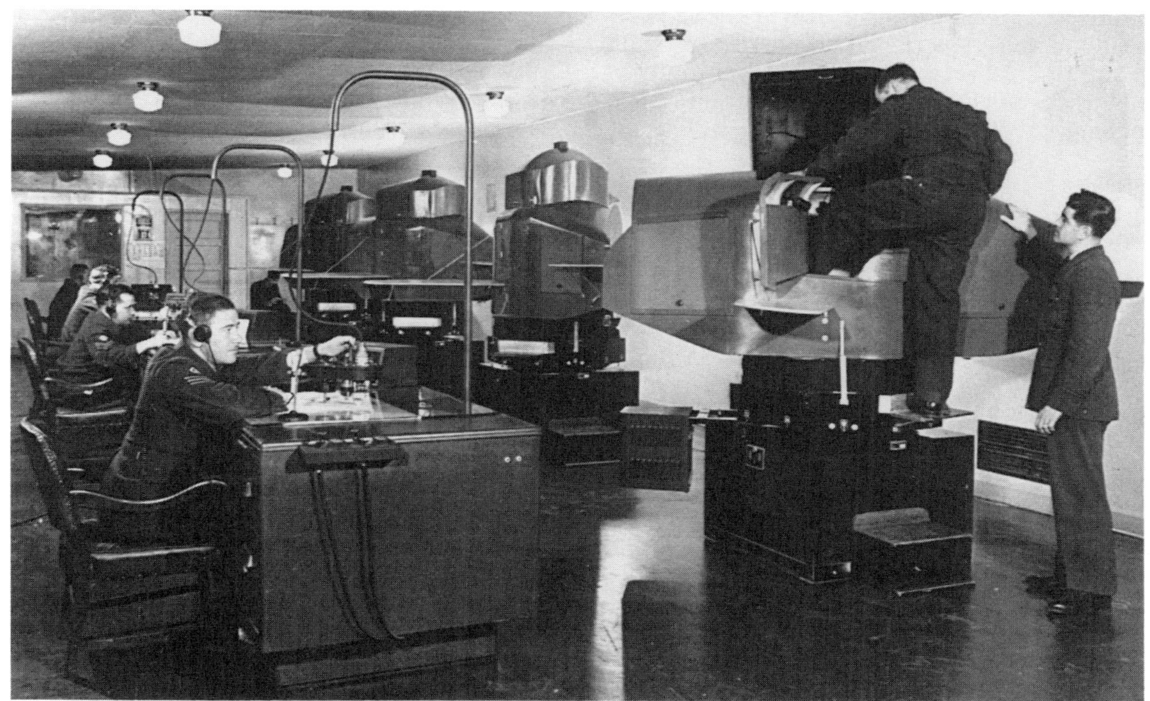

Before pilot trainees were allowed to fly aircraft, they were trained in Link flight simulators like these in Virden, Manitoba. In 1940 the number of hours spent in a Link was 5 hours, but that increased to 20 hours in 1941 and to 25 hours in 1943. (PMR 79–425)

Aircrew trainees at Virden, Manitoba, learn Morse code. (PA 140653)

take-offs, landing and navigation were allowed to "pass out" of elementary flying training. Twenty-two and a half percent failed to pass for reasons other than sickness, injury, or death.[9]

The Last Leg to the Wings

At the service flying training schools, there was an emphasis on precision flight. Students were expected to improve their navigational abilities with cross-country flights while drawing maps of towns, roads, bridges, railways, and other important landmarks. Trainees were also required to do instrument, night flying, and formation flying exercises. As well, the pilot candidates took part in simulated bombing raids.[10]

One of the most difficult adjustments for the trainees at the service flying schools was the change from the single-engined aircraft used at the elementary flying schools to the larger two-engined airplanes. Pat Coggins, a pilot, recalled that the first reaction to the twin-engined machines was that he "would never be able to fly that 'bugger'. It was too big."[11] A former BCATP flying instructor, Stan Morris, said: "Of course, there were many more instruments. In Elementary Schools, you learned needle, ball and air speed. That was all you needed. The needle showed you the speed you were going. The ball showed you that you had to keep above stalling. Once you were in a twin, you had two motors and you had to synchronize them so they were not bucking each other. It was certainly a step up".[12]

The difficulty with the twin-engined machines began on the ground, as Paul Heasman, a pilot who trained at the service

Graduates of the service flying training school at Vulcan, Alberta, parade on their graduation. (PMR 79–412)

Practising gunnery skills on an aircraft simulator at the bombing and gunnery school at Paulson, Manitoba. (FPA 128138355)

Members of the Royal Australian Air Force training to be observers by taking sun shots at the Rivers, Manitoba, school. (PL 3722)

flying school at MacLeod, recalled: "You were used to a single-engine aircraft where you could use the brakes to steer, keeping it on the runway, but when you got to the Ansons with their air brakes, they didn't want you to use them anymore than you had to. You had to try to keep the aircraft on the runway with the engines. If you used the brakes too much and the pressure in the tanks was below eighty pounds, you couldn't take off, you had to go back and pump up the air."[13] Despite this, Stan Morris said the "two engines gave you a much better sense of security because one of the first things your instructor did was shut off one engine and show you that you could fly on one engine. Mind you, you had to make adjustments to twins. But if you were in a Tiger Moth and your motor went, you had to find a field right away."[14]

If a pilot candidate succeeded in his training at the service flying training school and received his wings, the next step was to one of the various operational training units outside the Prairies. Once a pilot had attained a high enough level of proficiency, he would be transferred to full military operations.

There was one other place a successful pilot candidate could be sent. That was the instructor training schools. Successful pilots, who looked forward to beginning their tours of duty overseas, were often disappointed when the call came for them to report to the instructor flying training school at Vulcan, Alberta, or, later in the war, to Pearce, Alberta. Top graduates in the navigation course were also sent to an instructor course at the Central navigation school at Rivers.[15]

7

Hazards of War

With such large numbers of aircrew of all the different categories, and the frequent stunts pulled by exuberant students and instructors, one would expect that there would have been a high number of accidents, but this was not the case at all. The number of casualties of the Air Training Plan remained low throughout the war. The reasons for this were the experience that Canada had in air training and the increasingly improved technology during the Second World War.

Yet, when reading newspapers of the war years, one is struck by the large number of accidents reported. This may have been because of the public interest in such stories as well as the genuine concern that the host communities had for those who had an accident.

One flying instructor, Stan Morris, recalled what a friend's crash meant to him: "A young lad had gone out for his solo. We were cautioned at all times to never let air speed get below stalling point. At supper time, he hadn't returned. The instructors all took off and found his plane. He had attempted to circle a straw stack and had let his air speed down or had held off on a turn and had spiralled in. We had to get a hold of our corporal and pack his belongings and send them home. I think that was the first time that many of us realized that we were in a war."[1]

In most host communities, the local air training school remained news. Almost every event that occurred at the schools was reported in detail in the local newspapers. Newspapers also reported on the stunts that the airmen did. One such report of an instructor who performed a number of stunts without an accident read: "Last Tuesday morning about noon one instructor of No. 32 school got into a daredevilish mood, either because he was glad to leave or was disgruntled. Anyhow, at the controls, he did considerable hedge-hopping over buildings in town, sweeping down the vacant lot between *The Sun* and Imperial Hotel, flew under the overhead pedestrian bridge across CPR tracks, circled around the flour mill a few times on a steep bank and generally cavorted at low altitude. At a subsequent court martial at the camp, several citizens were called to testify as to what happened."[2]

Not all the reports were amusing. Another community newspaper carried a story about a student's forced landing: "With one engine not working an RCAF twin-engined training plane from Rivers, Man., made a forced landing on the field at No. 11 Service Flying Training School here about 11 o'clock last night damaging the undercarriage and a propeller." The report added: "According to information available the plane was being flown by Flying Officer McNaughton. One engine is reported to have gone dead and the landing here necessitated. In coming down on the unprepared field a deep bank of snow was struck and the damage done. . . . Complete information was not available but it is believed that the pilot was Gen. McNaughton's son who is known to be at Rivers."[3] There was no further report about the student nor confirmation that he was the general's son.

The Neepawa Press reported when a trainee's life was saved by Andrew Graham and Ross Bruce Francis, brothers who lived at Eden, Manitoba, that the two "received letters of congratulations from Hon. C. G. Power, Minister of National Defence for Air. . . . The letter stated that when an aircraft crashed in the field nearby, the two men removed the unconscious pilot from the burning plane at the risk of their own lives. Although smoke was streaming from the cockpit, the brothers disregarded personal safety and saved the pilot a few moments before the gas tank exploded, enveloping the aircraft in flames."[4]

Not all stories had such a good ending. A more typical article that appeared in the local papers was about the crash and the funeral of Robert Condie at the service flying school at Macleod in April, 1941. The ceremony included a three-volley salute by the firing party and included the playing of the hymn "Abide With Me" and ended with the sounding of the "Last Post." The body was then taken to the CPR depot to be taken to Condie's home at Crystal City, Manitoba. The *Macleod Gazette* reported that, "Among the hundreds that lined the streets and the CPR grounds were veterans of the Great War, North West Mounted Police . . . Railway officials and Town officials. . . . Before leaving to accompany his son's remains, Robert Condie Sr. . . . witnessed the ceremonial service, with head bowed in grief and accompanied by friends." The report added: "To him and the sorrowing wife sympathy of the entire personnel of No. 7 Station and Macleod and district citizens are extended."[5]

The Safety Record

Despite the frequency of such stories, when the statistics of the number of hours flown by the student pilots for every fatality are examined, it is clear that the Air Training Plan had an excellent record for safety. This record looks even better when compared to the number of fatalities exper-

These two Cessna Cranes crashed before getting airborne at Calgary on June 17, 1943. One of the two students swerved off his runway into the path of the other. Even though both of these aircraft were totally destroyed, neither of the students received any injuries. (PMR 81–139)

ienced during the air training scheme of the Great War in Canada:

Hours Flown Per Fatal Accident, the Great War and the British Commonwealth Air Training Plan[6]

The Great War		BCATP	
April, 1917	200	1940–41	11,156
May, 1917	1,000	1941–42	14,001
June, 1917	1,960	1942–43	1,725
December, 1917	1,500	1943–44	20,580
July, 1918	1,560	1944–45	22,388
August, 1918	3,300		
October, 1918	5,800		

The reason for the high number of fatalities during the Great War was that little was known about training pilots. The pupil in that war had only enough time with his instructor to learn how to take off and to land. Once the instructor believed the student had learned these two skills, he was allowed to teach himself the principles of flight. The technology of training had developed considerably by the Second World War, when pupils received much more dual training before being allowed to fly solo.[7]

The Second World War's impressive safety record was marred by increased fatalities in the 1942–1943 period that resulted from the pressure for more trained pilots brought on by the successes of German forces in northern Africa, the Allied losses at Dieppe, and the threat of the Axis invasion of Russia. Even by the time the United States entered the War after Pearl Harbor on December 7, 1941, the Allies had not made progress against the Axis. In 1942, the Allies called for more aircrew and stepped up war production. The pressure for more aircrew continued until the success of 1943 in northern Africa and the invasion of Sicily by the Allies.[8]

As one would expect, the local newspapers were full of accident reports in 1942 when the pace of air training was sped up. One example was the front page of *The Macleod Gazette* on July 30, 1942, which reported the crash of an Avro Anson during the night at the local school, the funeral of another airman at the RAF school at Pearce, and a spectacular midair collision of two aircraft that killed two pilot trainees and an

This Avro Anson aircraft crashed at Cardston, Alberta. The aircraft is being guarded by the RCMP officer sitting on the nose of the machine. (NA–5005–1)

instructor at Pearce. The paper reported that "two Stearman training machines collided, one report stated at about 200 feet above ground, one machine . . . falling into the river, the other crashing on the bank." In one aircraft, the "student pilot who was alone . . . tried to bail out, as the body was found some distance from his machine."[9]

During the period of increased accidents, an article in the *Weyburn Review* explained the situation best when it pointed out:

While the newspapers almost daily contain reports of fatal accidents happening to young Canadians or British airmen in training in this country for air battle to come abroad, the ratio of fatal accidents at training stations is relatively very small when the vastness of the air training program underway in Canada is studied.

When the fact is borne in mind that there are many scores of thousands of young aircrew men in training in the dominion, and that thousands of instructors accompany them on their training flights, the great marvel is that there is not a much greater percentage of fatal mishaps among the airmen in training. The official wastage anticipation in air training is placed at 15 percent, but the actual fatality percentage is much less than that figure, it may be pointed out.

When fatal accidents occur—and their occurrence is always a matter of regret to all and pain and sorrow in bereavement to relatives—the vast extent of the air training scheme should be borne in mind and the total brought into the reckoning of the number of students and instructors who take off daily at the training schools. From that standpoint, the logical one from which to view the score, the loss of human life at the airports is really remarkably small bearing in mind the highly hazardous nature of the work in hand in support of the Allies' war effort.

The victim of a flying accident at Yorkton receives full military honours. (RA 7118[8])

This was an accurate statement on the extent of air training accidents. The article correctly concluded, "Happy landings to the men in training at the airports, but if fatalities occur they must be looked upon as being incidents among the hazards of war".[10]

Although this article was accurate, it must be remembered that the writer was trying to calm the doubts in the communities during the period of the highest frequency of accidents. One aircraft instrument repair tradesman, A. S. Edger, remembered the grim feeling when accidents occurred: "In the five years that I was connected with the Air Training Plan, we had two fatal crashes; one in Regina and one in Winnipeg . . . both of them were at night. . . . At Winnipeg, we were out in the morning, while there was a gloomy bunch of people around there because we knew the pilot and we knew what happened to him."[11]

Pat Coggins recalled that when he was training at Regina, a fellow student was flying over the airport when he stalled and went into a spin. He did not pull up and crashed on the tarmac with his fellow trainees watching. "Right away, all trainees had to get into aircraft and fly. They always did that when they had a real bad crash. Don't give them time to sit back and think about it, especially when they're training and not too secure yet. If you have time you start thinking about what you are doing there, especially when you see it happen on the aerodrome."[12] Like Pat Coggins, trainees learned that although crashes had to be acknowledged, their training had to continue because there was a war on.

8

Operating the Plan

When the air training schools were established across the Prairies, the residents of the host communities became very close to the personnel. To a great extent, it was not the trainees who were known to the residents and involved in the daily cultural events of a community, it was the permanent staff. The trainees arrived for a month or two, then moved on. While they were there, the students had a huge task: training and learning. There was not enough time for them to interact with the surrounding communities. The permanent staff, however, were often involved in community life. The importance of the permanent staff to the communities was made clear in an *Estevan Mercury* article on the closing of a school on February 10, 1944:

> *It is a parting that brings many regrets not only in a community sense but in a personal sense as well, for not only have the men of the force established themselves in a high regard in the community but have made close friendships individually and not a few of the fine young ladies of Estevan have found their life-mates and will leave their homes here to go with their husbands to the homeland of these English boys. . . . these boys truly became a part of Estevan's community activity and their various talents and interests found expression in many ways which all helped to enrich our social life.*[1]

The permanent staff included service workers like kitchen workers, administrators, and aircraft repair tradesmen. Ground crews and station administrators were not the heroes, but they were vital to the smooth operation of the schools. The number of permanent staff was not small; the elementary flying schools had over five hundred while the larger service schools and bombing and gunnery schools varied from 1,100 to over 1,600 permanent staff. There could have been no heroes without them doing their jobs throughout the Plan in Canada and overseas.

Fulfilling a Vital Role

The role played by the ground crew was important but, to this point, very little recognition has been given to their contribution to the British Commonwealth Air Training Plan. Robert Collins, a well-known author and ground crew man during the war, pointed out that "RCAF ground crew have been almost ignored in histories of the war because, although their work was vital and some of them died in action, for the most part that work was undramatic. The best available book on the British Commonwealth Air Training Plan is devoted almost exclusively to aircrew. It fails to even *mention* the Technical Training Station at St. Thomas, Ontario, where 45,000 ground crew received final training."[2]

The work that the ground crew did was not glamourous and in some cases it was

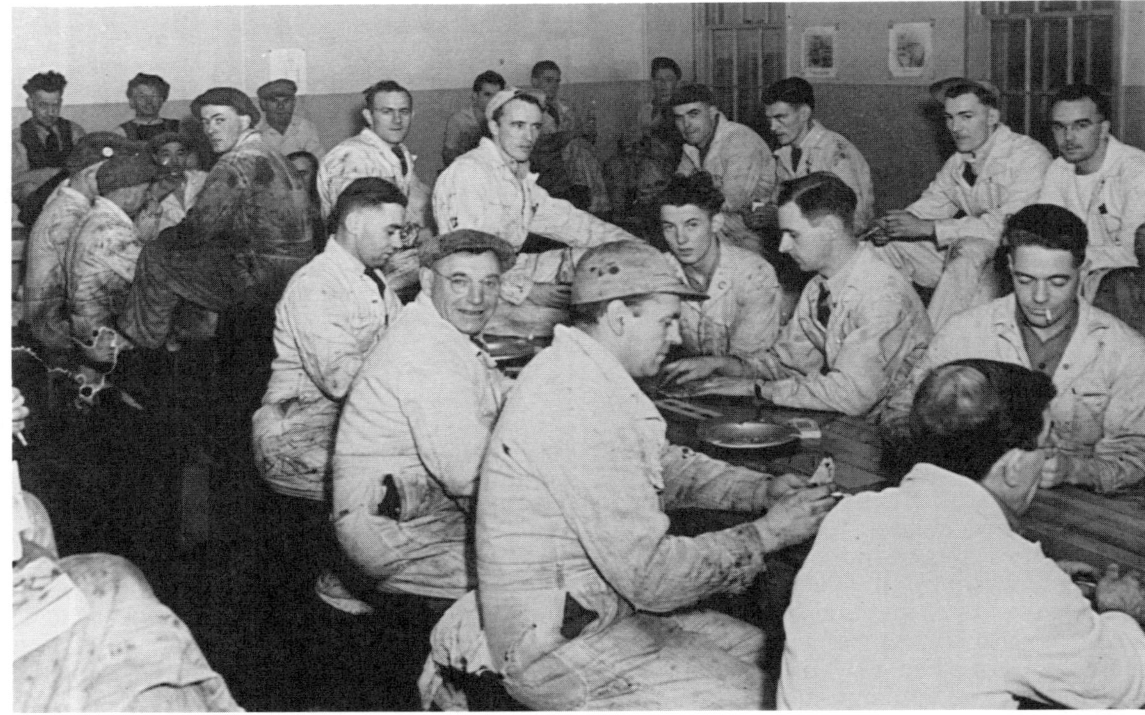

Maintenance workers in the cafeteria of a Manitoba air observer school. These were the men on the ground that kept the aircraft in the sky. (PAM, Gingras, Charles J. 94)

Members of the Women's Division refuel an aircraft. As the war went on, women took on more and more "men's work." (PAM, Gingras, Charles J. 38)

difficult and dangerous. Flying instructor Jim Kirk remembered that he "always felt sorry for a lot of our men on the line, even those that were more qualified and came out to start our aircraft for us. He would be there in thirty-, forty-below weather and would have to swing that crank standing behind the engine, winding that crank until the motor fired up. Then the blast from the propellor came. He would have to walk with his back to it and crawl under the aircraft to the other engine and crank that one, then get out by the tail." Kirk recalled how dangerous it was: "We did have one bad accident; one fellow slipped and got his head cut off by the propellor. He was behind the propellor between the aircraft and the engine, right by the leading edge of the wing."[3]

Another airman, Phil Ellison, said: "Our ground crew were there when you took off and they were there when we came back. They felt bad when an aircraft was lost. I talked to a lot of fitters and riggers. They wondered if they had done something wrong and the aircraft had failed. I think in the whole scheme of things we forgot who kept the aircraft going."[4]

On the air training stations, no service could be ignored. The RCAF had to establish dental clinics, general supply sections and kitchens, a supply system as well as a security section.

Against the Threat of Fire

One of the ground crew sections that was very important was the fire department. The *Yorkton Enterprise* reported that fire protection was of considerable importance. "Particularly during wartime when economy must be the watchword, it is sound logic to invest money in good fire-fighting equipment rather than suffer the huge losses which are often the result of fire."[5] The importance of fire protection was reinforced in the early years when fire caused significant losses such as the destruction of buildings at Mossbank. Another dramatic fire occurred on May 21, 1941, at the air observer school at Portage la Prairie. Only one week after hangar number two was finished and a dozen new aircraft had just been placed in it, a student pilot, flying at two hundred feet, stalled and crashed into it. The Anson aircraft inside the building had just been filled with fuel. In moments, gas tanks were exploding, making the hangar unapproachable. A wind had spread the flames to hangar number one, but it was saved.[6]

Action was taken in 1942 at the Mossbank and Dafoe bombing and gunnery schools to build swimming pools to supply the water storage needed to fight fires. These were the only schools on the Prairies to receive swimming pools for firefighting water supply.[7]

Motor Transport

Another large and important part of the ground services was the motor transport section. Motor transport was responsible for all trucks, cars, and tractors. The work included both the operation of these vehicles and their maintenance. The men of the section found themselves driving officers to town, driving large trucks with small cranes to crash sites to load up aircraft, and clearing snow in the winter. As well, tractors had to be used to haul planes out of hangars and muddy fields, and for road construction.

Added to these duties, the transport section was responsible for the maintenance and operation of the station's ambulance, although, as the *Yorkton Enterprise* noted, "The ambulances are under the authority of the medical officer and used for taking patients to hospital or for emergency work. During night flying an ambulance must be stationed at the hangars to be ready for an emergency, a driver standing by all through night-flying."[8]

Roy K. Cousins dispatches aircraft in the control tower at the air observer school at Portage la Prairie in 1942. (PAM Gingras J., 24)

Avro Anson Mark I aircraft await duty at a typical operations hangar at Edmonton. The one in the back is undergoing a thorough mechanical inspection. (JRA 015304806)

The Met

Vital to the continuous flying of the schools were accurate weather forecasts by the meteorology section. It was clear that it was "important for them to have an accurate picture of the present weather conditions in the surrounding country, as it would be extremely dangerous to send a young student flier on a cross-country flight without knowing whether or not he is likely to encounter storms, fogs, icing or other hazardous conditions."[9]

The meteorologists used teletype machines to keep close communication with other schools about the student flights. This section was also responsible for air traffic control. "Met" had to keep a record of all flights and departures, collect flight plans, and report the flights to the airports that the aircraft were travelling to.[10]

Keeping the Aircraft in the Air

Among service sections, maintenance was central to the training effort because it was responsible for keeping aircraft in the air. The three major areas of maintenance were air-engine, airframe, and air instrument. Maintenance was a large section of tradesmen working in specialized areas.

The regular work of the ground crew was the repairs of any aircraft that needed it, as well as a periodic complete check of the aircraft every forty flying hours. The procedure, known as the P-40, included inspection of the airframe, engine, aircrew, instrument, armament, electrical and radio equipment. The procedure required about six hours to complete.[11]

The safety of the pilots of the aircraft

Ground crew at Winnipeg hurry to assemble the newly arrived English Avro Ansons on November 19, 1940. (NMST 5886)

Mechanics at work on an aircraft engine at the Winnipeg air observer school. Some civilians look on as the ground crew demonstrate their trade. (FPA 128138347)

was central to the work of this section: "Upon the knowledge of the personnel carrying out these inspections depends the very lives of the pilots who fly the aircraft." The *Yorkton Enterprise* editorialized, "So you see the maintenance squadron of each RCAF station throughout Canada is really, as stated before, one of the most important cogs in the great wheel of air force operations." The newspaper concluded that, "It is the men on the ground who keep the aircraft in the air."[12] A good ground crew was indeed the core of a good training school.

The Women's Division

The recruitment of the ground crew was not a great problem for the RCAF. This was especially true once the air force began to call on the Canadian Women's Auxiliary Air Force, which was renamed the RCAF (Women's Division) in the spring of 1941.[13]

Don O'Hearn, a RCAF airframe tradesman, recalled that members of the Women's Division "were working in the fabric shops

Above: Members of the Women's Division at Macleod stand at the side of an Avro Anson with the engines running. (PL 6885)

Below: As more men had to go into aircrew training, members of the Women's Division expanded their areas of expertise. In this photograph, the WDs are doing maintenance on a vehicle. (PL 6965)

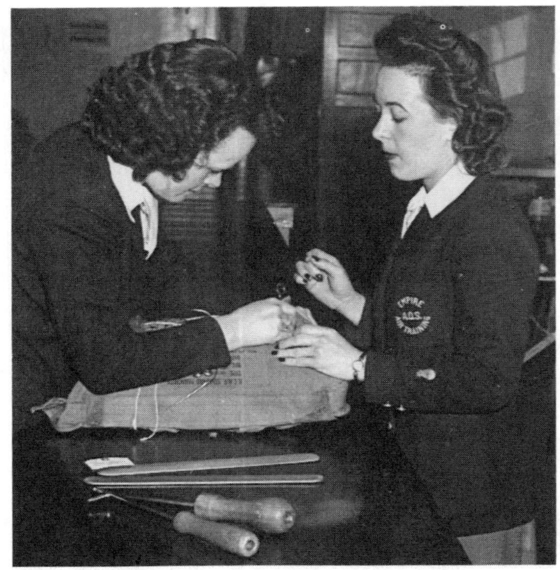

Members of the Women's Division pack parachutes at Portage la Prairie in 1944. (PAM, Gingras, Charles J. 30)

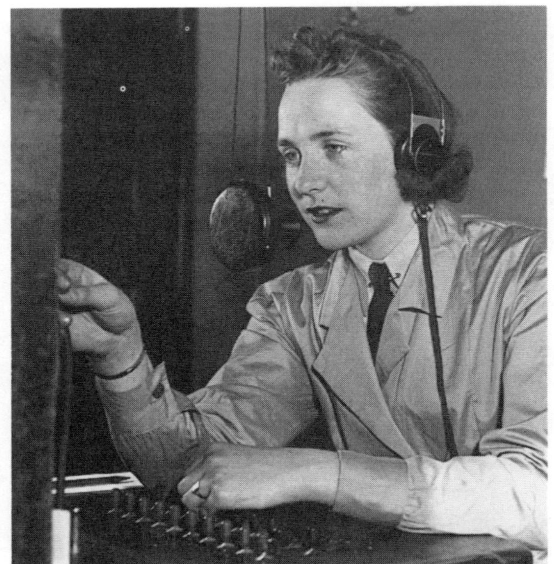

One of the traditional roles of the Women's Division was work on the telephone switchboard. This is a member of the WDs at the service school at Macleod, Alberta. (PL 6971)

as we called it then, packing parachutes, doing fabric work. They were in the clerical offices typing and that kind of thing." O'Hearn went on to say, "You see at that time, for women, it's not like today, there was no equal opportunity; women were relegated to what was known as a 'woman's job'. They drove trucks and vehicles and formed a service of flying airplanes into various fields. It was nothing to see a woman get out of a Spitfire or a Lancaster. They did a tremendous job in that regard."[14]

One member of the Women's Division, Dorothy Currie, recalled that: "On the whole, I would say the WDs were respected. There would be the odd airman who didn't like them, but on average, they were accepted."[15]

Indeed, it was both the men and women of the air force who kept the airplanes in the air. It was not surprising that the Women's Division motto was "They serve that men may fly." This motto was the central point of the 1943 recruitment campaign. The motto and the opportunity to contribute to the war effort doubled the number in the division and brought the total number of women to 14,562. They took training as instrument technicians, airframe and aero-engine mechanics and in other areas. With their participation, men whose aspirations to fly were thwarted by the need for ground crew were freed to train as aircrew.[16]

9

"The Tie that Binds"

The servicemen and women of the Air Training Plan were quickly integrated into the activities of the towns and cities near the schools. Despite the strains that resulted because of a housing shortage and wartime restrictions, good will prevailed on both sides. The aim of the RCAF was to have a full range of cultural and recreational activities within the training schools and within the host communities to promote high levels of morale and therefore better discipline in the schools.

Civilians in the host communities had to fulfill their own needs as well. The *Yorkton Enterprise* reported on December 20, 1941, that a Christmas concert was staged at the Roxy theatre by a civilian group in aid of the Enterprise Empty Stocking Fund, to supply needy children with Christmas gifts. It was also noted that, "The Canora Symphony under the baton of Egon Grams provided the backbone of the entertainment and when one considers how many of their orchestra they have lost through enlistments they presented a very fine show indeed and were full measure for the applause they received."[1] Orchestras, bands, and dramatic groups were ending their activities because many of the men and women who had been involved were no longer available. The airmen and airwomen were warmly welcomed when they pursued these activities in the communities.

A Club to Host the Airmen and Airwomen

A natural outcome of the interaction with the air schools was the establishment in many communities of hostess clubs and recreation rooms for the air force personnel. The towns located a place for the hostess rooms, as the *Souris Plaindealer* reported in 1942: "The managing board of the United Church in Souris has unanimously agreed to donate one of its church basements for the use of the airmen of the Souris Service Flying Training School No. 44 as a club room, when it opens this summer. The announcement was made by Wm. Coltman, chairman of the club room committee at a well-attended meeting of the recently organized Souris and District War Service organization on Thursday evening last. He moved that offer be accepted."[2]

Even cities as large as Winnipeg established hostess centres for airmen. The *Winnipeg Tribune* reported that: "Facilities for card games, checkers and other games which require little space to be played will be provided, as well as magazines, newspapers and overseas' papers for RAF men who have been sent to Canada to train."[3]

The amount of interaction between host communities and air stations varied across the Prairies. In general terms, the closer the

A group of instructors at Portage la Prairie relax on an Avro Anson aircraft. This particular aircraft was not airworthy and was used for ground instruction. (PAM, Gingras, Charles J. 41)

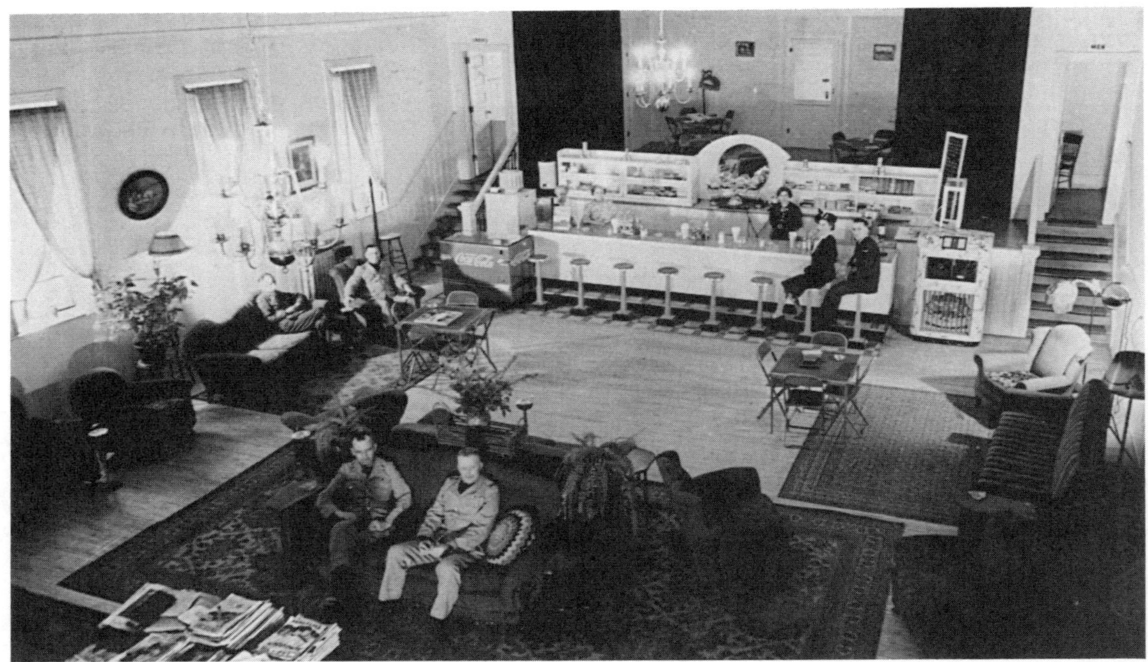

A view of the Yorkton hostess club, in 1941, set up by local women to offer airmen and airwomen an establishment in the town to visit. (RA 7168[2])

Men and women of the air force relax with some piano playing and ping-pong in the officers' mess at Yorkton. (RA 7112[3])

station was to the host community, the higher the level of involvement. This was made clear in the *Daily Diary* of the Dafoe bombing and gunnery school: "This being a somewhat isolated station, the social and recreation facilities have been developed to a very high degree within the station itself. In fact, it becomes very hard to find an evening that is not occupied with some social or recreational activity on the Station."[4]

The schools of the Air Training Plan that were the most isolated and therefore had the highest level of internal activity and a minimum of interaction with the nearest communities were the bombing and gunnery schools. This was seen throughout the different facilities. For example, libraries were established for the use of the servicemen on the base although they were never a center of activity. The Mossbank bombing and gunnery school boasted on April 9, 1941, of already attaining "a library of 1,017 books and [the use of] over 50,000 magazines since opening last September." The entry in the *Daily Diary* went on to claim that "over 1,000 sheets of writing paper and envelopes are used daily and about $35 worth of stamps are sold daily."[5] These claims may have been exaggerated, but the library filled an important role. In Neepawa, the library was a place "where students can read and write in quiet and comfort. All stationery and envelopes are supplied free of charge. The library contains 1,400 fiction and nonfiction books, as well as an average of one hundred magazines per week distributed. Eighty-five reference books as well as the educational courses provided, are given to help RAF students in their course."[6]

In some towns, such as Yorkton, Swift Current, and Assiniboia, library facilities were provided in the community through the local hostess clubs. In Swift Current, for example, appeals were made for material for the reading rooms at the service flying training school and the library in the hostess club. The libraries in the hostess clubs provided easier access to books than the local public libraries.

Parties

Parties were arranged to encourage interaction between air personnel and civilians in the communities. There were three kinds of parties: the small internal event for station personnel and, at times, small groups of civilians; the graduation event; and the external public relations event.

The first had a recreational value for the airmen on the stations. The internal gatherings were often a simple "party held in the officers' mess" or one of the other messes. These parties were often reported as events which included a "programme of singsong, stories, games, and moving pictures."

Graduation parties, which were sometimes held in the nearby communities, were celebrations for the graduates and often ended with a formal dinner. One example occurred when the elementary flying training school in Regina held a dinner at the Hotel Saskatchewan on September 30, 1943. The graduates and their instructors gathered at the hotel for a few short speeches and a rousing send off of the trainees to the next school. The air observer school in Prince Albert routinely held its graduating dinners at the P.A. Cafe in the city. In many other cases, though, the dinners were held on the station.[7]

The most common type of gathering was to open the station to the public for a party which usually ended with a dance or a film. The Claresholm air school paper, *Windy Wings*, reported: "The Men's Club monthly Airmen's party held in the IOOF Hall Friday night . . . drew the largest number of Airmen ever yet to avail themselves of this hospitality. . . . Karl Johnson's Swing Band went over big for dancing, and the boys really enjoyed the singsong. In fact the transportation outfit provided by the airport just about gave up hope of getting the boys out of the hall in time. . . . The success of this evening has encouraged the wavering committee to continue this form of hospitality."[8]

Silver Screens

Added to large events like carnivals and fairs were the routine screening of films at the air training schools. The Mossbank bombing and gunnery school reported the acquisition of a movie projector as "all to the good as there is real need for better entertainment at this station, being it is that

Even with the stress of training huge numbers of aircrew for the war, there was time to relax. At Yorkton, the crew enjoys an informal party. (RB 3570)

Members of the cast of an RCAF production of "Why Am I Always Joe?" at Yorkton belt out a song. (RA 7134[5])

we are somewhat isolated." With the installation of the projecting equipment, films became a regular recreational event. The North Battleford elementary flying training school reported, "The movie show continues to operate five nights in each week." Other schools, like the Dafoe bombing school, had six evenings of film entertainment a week.[9]

Some of the popular Hollywood films that were seen by the air personnel at the schools were *What's Buzzing Cousin*, the Walt Disney production, *Fantasia*, *Assignment to Brittany*, *The Heat's On*, *The Man From Down Under*, *The Rains Came*, *Mr. Deeds Goes to Town*, and *The Desert Song* starring Dennis Morgan and Irene Manning. War movies like *A Yank in the RAF* and *The Valiant Lady*, which starred Ginger Rogers and James Stewart, were also popular selections.

To the Stage

Stage productions on the stations, which reflected the abilities and interests of those who were involved in them, were useful in drawing schools and communities closer together. The productions ranged from amateur to "professional." Claresholm's *Windy Wings* reported a production on April 1, 1943: "Station talent was paraded for the approval of the personnel of No. 15 SFTS . . . acts which included vocal numbers, monologues, clown acts, hillbilly tear-jerkers and a quiz contest. . . . A cosmopolitan crowd, the artists were made up by RCAF, RAF and RAAF personnel. Prize winners of the evening were the three hillbillies from Rattle Snake Gulch."[10]

The *Penhold Log* reported a more "professional" production in August 1944: "Probably the last and perhaps the best of Penhold's stage shows was presented to enthusiastic audiences in the Recreation Hall. . . . This revue included the old favourites, notably the Atkinson-Ridley-Murgatroyd team, and at the same time disclosed such abounding new talent . . ."[11]

Other stations such as the elementary flying school at Davidson reported stage productions that included vaudeville, singing, dancing, jokes, and skits. Plays were also presented, often by dramatic groups on the stations. These groups were active in producing plays for both station personnel and the public events.[12]

There were several agencies within the armed services that provided dramatic productions at the air training stations. The RCAF had its own shows which toured the stations. These shows, like the local ones, included a variety of entertainment. Groups were formed by interested personnel in their free time, travelling to nearby air schools to stage their performances. One such event was reported in the *Neepawa Press*: "'Paulson on Parade' is the name of a hit show produced by the personnel of No. 7 B & G School Paulson. . . . It is a fast moving revue with excellent singing, dancing, music, and variety comedy is exceptionally good. . . . [the] Paulson swing band, under direction of Cpl. Hopburn, plays some smart numbers, and accompanies the show throughout the performance."[13] The air force shows included plays, skits, dancing, singing, and "swing time" band sessions. Other stage shows

Members of the fast-moving comedy, "The Mad Hatter's Review," from the Medicine Hat service school. (PMR 81–150)

were provided by the War Auxiliary Services. All these stage shows were held internally at the schools with few if any civilians in the audience.

Beyond the internal armed services stage shows, there were large numbers of shows staged by civilians at the stations. The Davidson elementary flying school reported a typical civilian group of entertainers on March 10, 1944: "A dramatic group from the University of Saskatchewan arrived from Saskatoon in the evening and put on the play 'The Male Animal' in the Recreation Hall. The play, a comedy, was a sensational hit, and the acting was extraordinarily well done." Another show reported at the bombing and gunnery school at Mossbank included entertainers from Moose Jaw and the local radio station CHAB.[14]

The stage shows presented to the host communities by the airmen and airwomen had a greater impact on public relations as demonstrated by the large number of prairie papers that gave prominent coverage to the events. The *Yorkton Enterprise* showed the community's enthusiasm and participation in its report about one stage show held on October 9, 1941: "Yorktonites turned out in full force Sunday evening to welcome the RCAF boys to the Roxy Theatre on Yorkton's Broadway. From a per capita point of view New York never gave warmer welcome to a cast on opening night on the Great White Way than Yorkton gave the airmen and it can also be said that no New York cast ever surprised or pleased their patrons more than 'the lads in greyish-blue.' Almost every seat in the vast auditorium was taken." This same kind of enthusiasm and numbers in attendance continued until the air training schools closed.[15]

The Swing Bands Came to Town

The Royal Canadian Air Force had a policy of having bands at all the air training stations. This often meant that the local schools provided bands to communities that had no band of their own. Swing sessions, concerts, Christmas music festivals, and community fund-raising events were often centred on the performance of one of the RCAF or RAF bands during the war period.

A typical event that one of the air force bands was involved in was reported by the *North Battleford Optimist*: "Mr. Colburn gave the entire proceeds of the dance attendance and checkroom takings, which is greatly appreciated by the North Battleford Red Cross Society, which must keep 'going on' to raise funds for the Red Cross . . . Snappy music was supplied by the Blue Aces orchestra, by permission of Group Captain A. P. Bett."[16]

The statement in *The Estevan Mercury* that "the station orchestra, whose good work is much in evidence on so many occasions at our dances, socials, concerts, etc., continues to move from one success to another," applied to the majority of Air Force bands in the West during the war years.[17]

The Yorkton service school had a close relationship with the community, beginning with the creation of the station band. The city of Yorkton had the instruments and the air training school had the desire to form a band. The *Yorkton Enterprise* explained the event: "Mayor Peaker recently visited No. 11 Service Flying Training School and learned, among other things, that the boys of the RCAF wish to start a band. The city has a number of band instruments out on loan and those who have these are asked to return them to the city office."[18] This early cooperation was followed by a continued enthusiasm among Yorkton residents for the public performances given by the RCAF band at the Roxy theatre. The same cooperation was reported in the *Winnipeg Tribune*: "Brass instruments for the organization of a band at the Royal Air Force Flying Training School at Carberry were presented to officers of the school at noon today on the floor of the Winnipeg Grain Exchange. The instruments, 16 in all, were purchased with donations made by a number of Exchange members."[19]

The Yorkton air school band on parade. In the background is the Roxy theatre where the band often played for the locals. (RA 7120[2])

Swing Time Dances

The same kind of cooperation that was seen in other areas of social interaction was also evident in regular dances. Even at the isolated bombing and gunnery schools, a significant effort was made to bring women to the dances. A *Diary* entry for May 1, 1942, at the Dafoe station stated that "the seventh Airmen's Dance was held in the Recreation Hall tonight with the usual large attendance present. Young ladies from the surrounding towns of Dafoe, Watson, Melfort, and Humboldt were brought to the station by private cars, and a very happy time was had by all. Music was supplied by the station orchestra."[20]

The *Diary* commented: "The Wet canteen is always closed on the nights of Airmen's Dance and soft drinks and other refreshments were served in the Small Canteen." This cautionary note, along with the statement that there was extensive participation by local women, was often repeated in the *Daily Diaries* of the air force training stations and local newspapers.[21]

The *Souris Plaindealer* reported that the local service school "held its opening dance of the year and swung into the seasonal mood with a Spring Frolic in the Drill Hall at the Souris airport last Friday. Over 1,000 were in attendance. Guests, officers and airmen crowded the occasion to swing to the music of the Brandon Manning Depot orchestra and the programme was spotlighted with an intermission floor show by members of the Souris Commando troupe."[22]

Airmen and members of the Women's Division dance at the New Year's party at the Yorkton school. (RA 7130[3])

Across the Prairies, news of the war crackled through the radios between tunes by Glenn Miller's swing band and the soothing songs of Vera Lynn; while it was reported at Portage la Prairie that "about 1,000 employees sat down to a banquet in No. 4 hangar. Dancing and refreshments were enjoyed by all on the Station. A most successful party. Actually 1,200 sat down to dinner, including many wives of staff members. The dance was held in the new drill hall, in the greatest comfort yet, Camp Shilo orchestra playing for the dancing."[23]

There were also a number of touring bands that provided swing sessions on the air stations. One of the most popular Canadian bands to tour the air training schools, was Mart Kenny and His Western Gentlemen. Don O'Hearn, an airframe mechanic during the war, remembered some concerts by "Les Brown, Guy Lombardo and other well known bands that came through. There was a lot of entertainment."[24]

Dorothy Minor recalled that, in Claresholm, Alberta, "Jitney dances" were held every night. "We loved them," she said. "Nobody had to pay at the door. The boys would buy tickets—10 cents. The dance floor was roped off after each dance, and another ticket was needed for the next dance. Needless to say, we girls were very popular. We danced with boys from Australia, New Zealand, Great Britain, and all across Canada and a few [from the] U.S. who had come north to join the RCAF. I loved to dance, and I loved every minute of the dances—not even minding that my mother and dad were waiting outside to drive me home."[25]

Alexandria (Macdonald) Miller, the Canadian bride of a British airman, remembered that "Partners were no problem—the men outnumbered the girls ten to one, so even the . . . widows came off their rocking chairs to join the dance circuit and had a ball doing it—even though the gossips were kept busy. . . . We learnt a lot from the fraternization with the British RAF. We were basically country bred kids [who] had not travelled far from home, while these [were] boys and men from a different country, [with] different ways and customs. Most had experienced war and the effects of war, whereas, for us, war was a word that meant ration books and watching for names on the 'Missing in Action' list but not the devastating thing that these boys had experienced."[26]

Pilot Bill Minor recalled that "the dances at Lethbridge were really something, I tell you. All these married girls would take their rings off and come to the dances when their *old man* was overseas. There was a lot of that. A lot of them knew each other for only a week or two, then got married. Then the old fella would have to go overseas."[27]

Romance

Local girls danced and laughed with the air trainees and air force personnel at social events. Local men and women played ball, hockey, and bingo with them. From the interaction of large numbers of air personnel with residents of the host communities came the marriage of local women to airmen. The obvious result of the marriage of local girls to airmen from Britain, Australia, or New Zealand was that one spouse would eventually have to leave his or her own country to join the other. Some Canadians, like Mrs. Miller, travelled to England to live with their husbands. Canadian women travelled to Australia, New Zealand, and other countries of the Commonwealth. On the other side, there were also many foreign airmen who liked the Canadian Prairies so much that they returned after their service in the war.

Weddings of airmen and airwomen were common. The *Daily Diary* of the service flying training school at North Battleford reported on April 29, 1944, the wedding of Airwoman M. W. Overend to Leading Air Craftman H. J. Plant. The entry in the *Diary* went on to comment that "Plant is an under training pilot from Herberton, Australia, and Overend is a member of the Station Accounts Section. The marriage took place at the Roman Catholic Rectory. . . . A reception was afterwards held at the Odd Fellow's Hall. The happy couple are honeymooning in Saskatoon."[28]

Dorothy and Ken Currie were another couple brought together by the war. Dorothy was a member of the Women's Division working as a telephone operator at Yorkton, where Ken was a flying instructor.[29]

The concluding report of the British Commonwealth Air Training Plan Supervisory Board stated: "In many cases, airmen formed permanent ties with Canada, which will remain through succeeding generations. More than 3,750 members of the RAF, RAAF, RNZAF, and Allied nationals under RAF quotas married Canadian girls."[30]

The Familiar Purr of Engines

The RCAF policy of integrating air personnel into the surrounding communities was very successful. This may have been a significant factor in the enthusiasm the people in the West had for the air force. The communities felt they were united with the air force in the war effort. As one air gunner, Phil Ellison, recalled, "The general feeling was that we had to get the people trained and this war won."[31]

The acceptance of the Air Training Plan in towns and cities across the Prairies was suggested by the high level of enlistment by local men and women into the RCAF. Statistics compiled by Greenhous and

Airwomen on parade at Yorkton. (RA 7121[2])

Hillmer, two historians from the Department of National Defence, demonstrate that prairie men enlisted in the Royal Canadian Air Force at a proportionately higher rate than men from any other region in Canada. The rate for Saskatchewan was only slightly below 50 percent of the number that had enlisted in the Canadian army. The province of Manitoba showed a rate of over 47 percent, while Alberta was over 43 percent.

When Greenhous and Hillmer gathered the statistics for enlistments across Canada, they found that RCAF was even more popular among the women of the western provinces. Saskatchewan was the only province in Canada that had more women enlisted in the Women's Division of the air force than in the Canadian Women's Army Corps. Alberta women's rate was nearly 91 percent. In Manitoba, the rate was 69 percent. The two historians concluded: "This last result seems most significant when it is remembered that recruiting for both women's services only began in the summer of 1941, when the Air Training Plan operation in the province was getting into top gear."[32]

A. S. Edger, an aircraft instrument repairman, recalled one attraction for many prairie boys to enlist was that the Training Plan "gave a lot of the fellas a chance to get off the farm where they sat for ten years just eking out a living. They saw some of the world."[33]

For those local boys who were too young to enlist, there was a growing cadet movement. Interest among local residents as well as widespread support for the cadet movement was evident in many of the air training schools. In July 1941, the Rivers *Gazette* noted the local enthusiasm for the air cadet movement: "Enquiries are coming into headquarters evidencing the enthusiasm of boys all across Canada in our cadet movement. 'It is this keen interest of the boys that has been responsible for the development of the scheme,' stated Flight Lieutenant Frost. 'The League is patterned after a proven organization, the Air Cadet Defence Corps of the United Kingdom, which was started before the war. Through this organization there are now 190,000 boys taking aviation training in Great Britain.'"[34]

The Swift Current *Sun* printed a retrospective article when the local school closed in March 1944 that illustrated both the economic benefits the air school had brought the community and the good will that was evident between the community and the air personnel:

There is no doubt the air school in Swift Current brought a lot of money directly and indirectly to the community: it helped to make business flourish in an already war-inflationary upsurge in which producers all round made more money and therefore had more to spend. It would be sheer hypocrisy to disguise the fact that people wanted the school to continue, for one thing, because it was good business. On the other hand the thousands of men from various parts of the Empire—who came and went as the courses were trained and graduated—brought something to Swift Current in the nature of "the tie that binds."[35]

The close relations described in the *Sun* came about because the RCAF directed local stations to participate in recreational activities of the local communities to help with the morale of the air personnel. The communities, for their part, were suffering from a loss of people because of enlistment and wartime migration. The needs of the communities and the training schools were complementary to each other.

The acceptance of the Air Training schools was indicated in an editorial in the *Weyburn Review*: "People in Weyburn who a few months ago found it difficult to sleep because of the unfamiliar drone of training planes overhead, are like the child accustomed to being rocked to sleep—they now find it difficult to get to sleep without the familiar purr of engines in the sky."[36]

10

Sharing Field and Ice

In communities across the Prairies, airmen and airwomen took the place of absent locals who had participated in sports before the war. The most important sports were those that allowed the most participation—hockey and baseball. Canadian airmen and airwomen who were familiar with these sports found they were quickly accepted in the host communities' activities.

The community's need was illustrated by a column that appeared in the Saskatoon *Star Phoenix* in July 1940. After describing the departure of a large number of men from Sonningdale, the columnist added: "The baseball team is facing difficulties since so many players have enlisted. Manager J. Atkins had his hands full rounding up substitutes to enable the team to play at Radisson on Dominion Day. However he succeeded so well that the Pats won first money. One former player, Chester Padget, who is home on leave from the navy, rejoined the team for the day and proved that he still knew how to play ball."[1]

Golf

Golf was another sport local communities and the air personnel enjoyed together. In the 1942 golf season, *The Estevan Mercury* reported that "a brisk sale for . . . books of golfing coupons available at 15 tickets for $3.00 with each ticket good for nine holes of golf. . . . It will find particular favor among the divotdigger at No. 38 SFTS and should bring the club some badly needed extra revenue without which it will not be able to carry on."[2] In Rivers, it was reported that the president of the golf club was to arrange a tournament and invite the RCAF.[3]

Swimming

Although there were a limited number of swimming pools on the Prairies during the war, a keen interest was shown among the men and women of the air force. The swimming activities ranged from the basic learn-to-swim classes to a number of swimming competitions in larger communities. The most significant swimming activities were summer competitive swim meets in which RCAF personnel participated. There were both interstation meets and meets held with prairie communities. One swimming competition was reported during the summer of 1944 in the *Souris Plaindealer*: "With flashy Bob Chipperfield stroking in championship form, No. 17 SFTS swimming team placed four firsts and two seconds in the area meet held in the Kiwanis pool at Brandon on Tuesday afternoon to . . . [come] through as best in the 50 yard freestyle and backstroked the same distance for first spot over the entrants from Rivers, Brandon and Macdonald."[4] The air station competitions were a part of a circuit sponsored by the RCAF that ended in finals at Winnipeg called the Command Swimming Meet.

Another form of swimming competition air force personnel participated in was the provincial summer circuit. The Mossbank bombing and gunnery school reported success at this level of competition in the summer of 1943: "The swimming team visited Saskatoon, Saskatchewan to take part in the Provincial Swimming Meet. In spite of a cold raw day—and colder water—the boys made an excellent showing against ranking swimmers."[5]

Swimming was also reported at the summer fairs. One such event was staged in the Souris River at Estevan. *The Estevan Mercury* presented the pending event with enthusiasm and an invitation for residents of the city to participate:

Don't be surprised if the old Souris River turns into whipped cream or maybe butter along toward sundown next Sunday. The ancient stream is in for one of the biggest churnings of its career the afternoon when more than 100 swimmers and divers of all ages and sizes will take part in the annual Water Sports of Estevan Branch Canadian Legion at Woodlawn Park.

About 40 airmen from Wing Commander Nathan and Flying Officer Brown right down the line, have already filed their entries for the RAF events and more are expected to come forward. Corresponding interest is being shown by aquatic stars of the town, and of course there will be a whole school of minnows in the youngster's contests. . . . A special feature will be an exhibition of diving by the young Edmonton star, LAC Allen Rudolph.[6]

Boxing and Wrestling

Boxing and wrestling were popular sports with the airmen. Boxing bouts were often internal station affairs. Interstation competitions as well as events with army and navy teams were also held. These events were open to spectators of the surrounding districts. Boxing, like swimming, followed a circuit that ended at the finals, the Command Boxing Championships. Wrestling was often the entertainment during the intermission between the boxing events.[7]

The interest in boxing was illustrated by the press coverage it received throughout the war. A typical report of a boxing match was found in *The Neepawa Press*: "A small crowd gathered at the arena Monday night to witness some very fine boxing by members of the Carberry RAF. The program, sponsored by the Lions Clubs in aid of underprivileged children, consisted of ten bouts of good clean boxing and displayed great sportsmanship throughout."[8]

On the Inside Track

Track and field sports did not play as large a role at the air training stations. As in the other sports, people from the host communities were invited as spectators to the station events. In the summer of 1943, the Rivers *Gazette* reported: "The third annual Track and Field Meet of No. 1 Central Navigation School was held on Thursday, August 19, and with ideal weather prevailing, it was the most

Under the warm skies of summer, Yorkton airmen and the local community compete together in a field day. (RA 7114[2])

successful yet. . . . A long list of events was run off, covering all phases of sport, and keen competition resulted. The station boasted some real athletes in its personnel."[9] Sports days across the Prairies were centered on track and field events that were familiar to all airmen.

Often, the sports days, which were held at the airport, included more than just sporting events. One sports day at the Swift Current airport reported in *The Sun* included an evening of social activities: "The first big public 'splurge' since [the] opening of No. 39 SFTS of the Royal Air Force has been set for Wednesday . . . and it promises to be a gala day to be remembered. There will be everything from a track meet to dancing, with festivities ending well after midnight. The public will be invited to enjoy this day of entertainment through invitation . . . so tell your friends at No. 39 that you'd like to attend."[10]

The Imports

Although there were sports like track and field that were common to Australian, Canadian, and British airmen, there were some sports that were not. Athletics engaged in by some British airmen were at best spectator sports for the civilians in the host communities.

Tennis, soccer, and cricket appeared to arouse limited interest in western Canada. Tennis, which allowed for some civilian participation, had value as a demonstration sport. Because courts were often available on the training stations, there was no need for the air personnel to seek tennis clubs in the communities. The tennis courts on the stations were low quality, built on skating rinks after the ice melted. The *Calgary Herald* reported that: "There will also be two hockey rinks built outdoors, and these will be turned into tennis courts in the summer."[11] In Rivers, *The Gazette* reported that the "Rivers Tennis Club will begin the season's play this week. An invitation has been extended to the Kenton Club, and through Ray Scott, YMCA to the boys in the RCAF men, to take part in friendly competitive games on Saturday, May 24th, afternoon and evening. It is expected the courts will be in good shape by that time."[12] The report was more recognition than tennis received in the majority of local newspapers across the Prairies.

Participation in soccer occurred at two levels for the air personnel: intersquadron games and competitions in the services leagues across the western provinces. The games played for the services leagues were also seen as demonstrations of the sport for the public. One typical game was reported in the *Penhold Log* in the summer of 1944: "By winning the first half of the Alberta Services Soccer League, Penhold Fliers have ensured themselves a place in the final deciding matches. Since then they have taken a resounding beating from an RAF, Carberry team, in a 'friendly' game, and have suffered their first defeat at the hands of a Canadian team when they lost to A-20. . . . Postings may be expected to deplete the Fliers' stock of regular first team players, but we still feel reasonably confident of taking the championship for the third year running."[13]

Although soccer was not popular among residents of the western provinces, there was enough interest in the sport for the formation of the provincial services leagues and for exhibition games. This same support was never attained by those British airmen who pursued cricket, however. Few matches were held and there were even fewer exhibition games given in the host communities. A report of a cricket match in the Swift Current *Sun* made it clear that this sport was unknown on the Canadian Prairies: "Besides the regular list of track and field events in the afternoon, the day will be climaxed with a cricket match between North of England and South of England in the evening. This will be an event of unusual interest for Canucks around these parts who have heard of but never saw a cricket match; it will bring a feeling of nostalgia to English-born folks living on these plains who have never seen this game since they left their homeland."[14]

Attempts were made throughout the war to establish a formal cricket league, but only small station leagues were formed. The RAF school at Moose Jaw found that by the summer of 1944 there was no longer any interest in the community nor in the other air training schools. Team members had to look to other more popular sports or look elsewhere for challenges. They chose the latter and travelled to Victoria and Vancouver for a series of matches.[15]

Basketball

A popular sport in western Canada was basketball. Teams of the best players were organized into station teams that played against other stations. Informal station and interstation basketball leagues were soon formed. The enthusiasm for this sport was reflected in Claresholm's *Windy Wings* when it reported: "The basketball season is nearly over as far as the station team is concerned, except for a few exhibition games that are trying to be arranged. The team was flying high in the Southern Alberta Senior League, but ran into considerable bad luck when it lost two regular players. . . . but the team did better than was expected in the league play-off with Macleod. In a close game in our Drill Hall, Macleod won the first game 40–33. In the second game at Macleod, our team was slightly disorganized and was beaten quite handily, 51–18."[16]

Members of a basketball team at the Yorkton school. (RA 7116[2])

In many sports, the members of the Women's Division had limited participation, and limited notice was made of them in the station *Diaries* and the local press. However, this was not the case with basketball. The *Davidson Leader* reported: "The W.D.'s from . . . Davidson defeated . . . Saskatoon, 15–12 in No. 2 command basketball championship semifinal in a rough, but good game. They are now eligible to travel to Winnipeg for finals [to play] Winnipeg. The winners will play at 7:00 o'clock for the grand championship."[17]

Chasing Pucks

Although basketball was widely appreciated in western Canada, the central winter sport remained hockey. Residents of the local communities looked to the service men to provide hockey entertainment. The most significant contribution that the schools of the Air Training Plan, army, and naval reserves made to western Canadian hockey occurred when formal leagues made up of service teams replaced civilian teams.

Before the war broke out, Manitoba's senior hockey league had been undergoing change because large numbers of local players were accepting positions on new hockey teams in England. The popularity of hockey as a spectator sport in Britain was increasing after the winter Olympics at Lake Placid in 1932. Although many in Britain knew how the game was played, few attempted it. While the best players from Manitoba accepted positions in Britain, the professional teams were calling on top junior players to take their places. The caliber of hockey was in decline as the war approached.[18]

The weakened hockey league collapsed with the declaration of war. It became a service league in 1940 when the Royal Winnipeg Rifles, Cameron Highlanders, HMCS Chippewa, RCAF Bombers, and other teams were formed. The Royal Winnipeg Rifles won the championship of 1940 and 1941. By 1943, it was widely believed that the caliber of Manitoba hockey was NHL level. In that year, the RCAF Bombers went to the Allen Cup championship in Ottawa, facing the Commandos, but did not bring the cup home. With the end of the 1943–44 season, the senior hockey league ended. It had to wait until after the war to be organized again.[19]

Yorkton was the centre of interest in the Saskatchewan Senior Hockey League because of the high standing of the Yorkton Terriers. In the fall of 1941, the Terriers were having difficulties created by the loss of players because of enlistments and wartime migration. The Terriers made it to the finals only to be eliminated. The *Yorkton Enterprise* was quick to note: "No sooner had the Yorkton Terriers been eliminated from the Saskatchewan Hockey League than they were confronted with a challenge from No. 11 SFTS hockey team for the right to the championship of Northeastern Saskatchewan."[20] The airmen from the local service flying training school were defeated in two straight games in a series of three. The games received much attention as the players from the air training station had gained the respect of the community.[21]

The collapse of the Saskatchewan Senior Hockey League that had been forecast in 1941 came in the fall of 1942. The league held a meeting in October and called for officials from the Canadian armed services to consider the formation of a senior services hockey league to replace the collapsed Saskatchewan league. The RCAF from Prince Albert, Saskatoon, and Yorkton, representatives of the army in Regina and Moose Jaw, and Flin Flon's essential war industry agreed to supply teams.[22] In Yorkton, players from the service school and the remainder of the Terriers formed the new local team, the Yorkton Flyers.

The Flyers, who were victorious over the Regina army team in their first game, were accepted by Yorkton as their own. Even though the airmen went back to interstation play afterwards, the airmen's participation in the hockey league was important during the turbulence of the war.

The fortunes of the Yorkton Terriers and the Saskatchewan Senior Hockey League did not improve after the 1942–43 hockey season. The fate of the league was clarified by *The Yorkton Enterprise* in its announcement on December 2, 1943: "Shortly after noon today the Yorkton Terriers Hockey Club issued a statement announcing their retirement from the Saskatchewan Senior Hockey League." The article went on to tell what would replace the league in Yorkton: "This does not mean that Yorkton will be without hockey, however, as No. 11 SFTS has entered a team in an interstation league and will play all their home games at the Front Street Arena." Hockey remained an important sport in the community and a significant activity that bound the civilians and the airmen of RCAF school closer together.[23]

As in Manitoba and Saskatchewan, in Alberta hockey teams turned to the three services to keep the senior league alive during the war. With the successful championship between the Luscar Indians and the Medicine Hat Tigers in 1942, increased involvement of the armed services was pursued with teams like the Edmonton Manning Depot, which went to the 1943 championship but lost to the Calgary Buffaloes. Finally, in the championship of 1944, the Prince Albert M. and C. Warhawks won the cup. In 1945, the Canmore team brought the cup home.[24]

The Game of Summer

Baseball remained one of the most significant sports in community relations with the air training stations because it attracted many participants and spectators. There were no formal leagues established across Saskatchewan for softball or fastball as there had been for hockey. This was one factor which made the sport more easily integrated into the daily activities of the communities. No other sport had more entries in the station's *Daily Diaries* than baseball, beginning early in spring with practices and intersquadron games. Soon, the reports were of interstation games. Teams that formed on the stations were soon involved with games that went beyond the closest communities.

Baseball, like basketball, allowed for a high level of participation by the Women's Division. The Women's Division softball teams found a large number of opportunities to play against other women's teams. The *Diary* of the air school at Davidson recorded one of the numerous events in the summer of 1944: "Our 'Winkos' (W.D. softball) visited Eyebrow and ran into some very stiff opposition. They took Bridgeford 1–0 in the first game but were nosed out by Mawson in the final by a score of 6–5."[25]

The press in the host communities was very active in reporting baseball regardless of whether the games were played between stations or between a local team and the station. In the summer of 1942, the Swift Current *Sun* reported: "Softball fans are getting . . . the RCAF team from Mossbank to meet No. 39 SFTS here in a double header at Westend park on Wednesday, with games starting at 3 P.M. and 7 P.M. The local air force team advanced into the second round by eliminating Caron EFTS on Saturday 11–5 and 6–1. It is three seasons since local fans sat in on a softball play-off and a large crowd is expected to turn out."[26] In Neepawa during the summer of that same year, *The Neepawa Press* reported a set of games that were in a Southern Manitoba League: "In the Brandon District Services Athletic Association, No. 35 EFTS, Neepawa played its first home game against No. 2 Manning Depot." The game was "a nip and tuck battle. . . . In the first of the 7th, Neepawa made several errors and nearly lost this lead, but hung on to win 14 to 12."[27]

Although baseball was significant in the communities during the war, the British airmen of the Royal Air Force were not interested in the sport. In the spring of 1943, *The Estevan Mercury* reported: "Facilities for the playing of Canadian summer sports will be maintained, with

Members of the very active Yorkton air school baseball team. The team participated in games with other stations as well as with many civilian teams. (RA 7115)

matches of baseball and softball throughout the coming season, and we are hoping that this will attract the mutual interests of RAF personnel."[28] This hope was never fulfilled. The *Diary* for the service flying training school at Moose Jaw reported in the summer of 1944, under the heading of *Fast Ball*, that "this game holds very little interest for English boys."

The nonparticipation of British airmen in baseball was another example of the cultural diversity that led to isolation of the RAF schools from the Canadian host communities.[29] Sports had an important role in the relations that had developed between the air training stations and the nearby communities, with airmen and airwomen taking the roles left vacant when local residents enlisted or moved away to work in essential industries elsewhere. Service personnel and local residents participated in those sports they knew, allowing Canadian air force personnel to integrate into the communities. At the same time, British personnel unfamiliar with Canadian sport were not as fully accepted.

11

Zoot-Suiters and the Yellow-Bellied

"Yellow-bellied English bastards," was the reply that local youths had to the heckles of British airmen stationed at the Moose Jaw Royal Air Force school. "Zoot-Suiters" was the name the Royal Canadian Air Force investigators called the civilian youths involved in the violence of 1944. There were several causes for the violence that erupted between the airmen and local youths. One was that the airmen had a long history of poor discipline, low morale, and a negative attitude toward the civilians of Moose Jaw. These problems were exacerbated by lower levels of interaction between the community and the Royal Air Force personnel.

The disturbances at Moose Jaw demonstrated the potential for conflict between air training schools and nearby communities during the Second World War. Yet, conflicts between prairie communities and the RAF and RCAF schools were rare. Only Moose Jaw reported any disturbances of this kind.

Not long after it opened, the service flying training school was no longer news in the *Moose Jaw Times-Herald*. Compared to other newspapers on the Prairies, the *Times-Herald* had significantly less coverage of the local air school. The impact of the school on the economy, however, could not be denied. The city had the benefit of the large school itself, with between 1,500 and 2,000 personnel, as well as the bombing and gunnery school at the nearby community of Mossbank. It also had one of the most significant British Commonwealth Air Training Plan repair depots in western Canada, operated by Prairie Airways, that employed one thousand people, most of whom were residents of Moose Jaw.[1]

Unlike the schools in communities such as Weyburn, Yorkton, or even communities as large as Saskatoon, the Moose Jaw RAF school participated in few sports and cultural activities in the community. The men's choir from the school performed often and the station band participated in some of the local "swing sessions." Yet, Moose Jaw residents were as likely to witness performances by the band from the initial flying training school in Regina, or the band from the Assiniboia school as performances by Moose Jaw personnel. The Moose Jaw RAF school, like the one at North Battleford, sought games of cricket as far away as Vancouver and Victoria. These games were of interest to the airmen, but did not benefit the city of Moose Jaw. In North Battleford, however, air personnel participated in other sports and cultural activities more often than air personnel in Moose Jaw, allowing for more interaction with the community. Although there were events like dances with airmen from the school in attendance in Moose Jaw, there were a lower number of cultural exchanges between the school and the community when compared to other communities across the Prairies. The reason for this was a condescending attitude toward the local residents on the part of the permanent British personnel.

The station was already isolated from the community when the new Commanding Officer, Group Capt. E. J. George, took over the school in 1943, and he inherited a discipline and attitude problem. The historians Greenhous and Hillmer argued that, unlike the commanding officer before him, George lived on the station. They believe this made him unsympathetic to the social needs of the host community, leading to the further isolation of the school.[2]

A Point of View

With the arrival of British airmen at Moose Jaw in 1940, it was apparent they brought with them a poor attitude. A report issued about the arrival of the RAF airmen in 1940 by personnel at training command in Regina warned that "few [of the British arrivals at Moose Jaw] appreciated fully the measure of co-operation that has prevailed between the RAF and the RCAF in the provision of the SFTS at Moose Jaw, and expressed a desire to learn more about the British Commonwealth Air Training Plan."[3]

The poor attitude was illustrated throughout the pages of the air training school's publication, *Prairie Flyer*, in articles that indicated the personnel's condescending attitude toward the local residents. In one article, LAC J. H. Martin urged his fellow countrymen not to assume that the Prairie was "a cultural desert. That Moose Jaw is not intellectually benighted is suggested by its possession of seventeen educational establishments—fifteen schools and two business colleges. Even if the curricula were bad, the teachers hopeless, and the pupils unteachable, we could at least acknowledge the nobility of the intention." In another article, he wrote, "Eating in the cafes to jukebox jive, we may fail to realize that there are people in the city who care deeply for the best in music."[4]

In addition to a poor attitude, some British airmen had a disciplinary problem. Under the heading of *Discipline* in the 1941 report by training command on the Moose Jaw air training school, it was reported, "Crime is not as prevalent on this Station now as it was in England."[5] Added to this, there were few transfers of personnel from Moose Jaw to other schools. This meant that the airmen with the disciplinary problems remained at Moose Jaw even though it was RAF policy to transfer personnel who caused trouble. No official reason was given for not transferring the men. The only action taken was a continuation of strict discipline at the school.[6]

In addition to the poor attitude and discipline, productivity was low in terms of aircraft serviceability, which was 10 to 15 percent below the average of similar schools across Saskatchewan. There was also a problem with hygiene. When Group Captain George arrived, he found an infestation of cockroaches in the mess hall, which had to be closed for two days so that cyanide gas could be used to kill the insects.[7]

The new commanding officer's goal was to establish air force standards which had never been attained at Moose Jaw.

Changes by George to correct the excesses that had occurred under the previous commanding officer, N. E. Mornison, resulted in a mutiny. The orders the new commanding officer published on July 15, 1943, included "withdrawing sleeping out passes from all airmen other than those authorized to live off the station; . . . providing that duty to duty passes would not be granted to airmen below the rank of Sergeant; and providing that plain clothes may not be kept on the station or worn on the station when proceeding from barracks to the main gate on leave or pass." These measures curtailed privileges that "were not only in excess of those permitted under RCAF regulations but were in excess of those laid down for the RAF."[8]

The result of these changes to the air personnel's privileges was seen the next day, July 16. In the morning, between 150 and 200 men of the maintenance wing "failed to appear on the morning working parade and marched around the camp encouraging other airmen to come out of the barracks and join them." The station warrant officer ordered the strikers back to work, but they refused. With George off the base, the acting commanding officer spoke to the men and they returned to work. When George returned to the station, he decided to suspend his new orders until a decision on further action was made. The maintenance wing continued to work following this decision.[9]

Court-Martialed

Following an investigation, George remained at the air school with his orders reinstated. Those deemed the leaders of the mutiny were court-martialed. The problem of poor discipline had been corrected, yet the issues of the isolation of the school, poor productivity, and low morale continued.[10]

Another investigation reported that civilians had no knowledge of the mutiny. Employees of hotels, barber shops, restaurants, and retail stores that benefited from the patronage of the air school were interviewed. Most told the investigator that relations were favourable.[11] However, one civilian, an English immigrant who worked on the local air training station, reported that "the service personnel of the above unit were the most insufferable grumblers, at anything and everything in general, that he had ever had the misfortune to be associated with. He further went on to say there were times when their grumbling, discontented manner made him feel almost ashamed of them as his countrymen."[12] This informant also described a situation where the members of the station's officer staff tacitly allowed abuses of the rules. The officers on the station appeared to be sympathetic or unable to act in opposition to the views of the leaders of the mutiny.[13]

The solution of court-martialing the leaders and imposing strict rules on the air training station did not change the attitudes of those who remained. High productivity, high morale, and positive attitudes could not be created by orders. The failure of the "solutions" to the 1943 mutiny was obvious one year later when violence erupted between airmen and youths in Moose Jaw.

Trouble between the two groups began on September 9, 1944, and continued for five nights. RAF personnel from the school taunted local youths, asking where their patriotism was, and if they had "cold feet or flat feet." The youths, the majority of them too young to enlist, responded by calling the airmen "yellow-bellied English bastards." Soon, fights broke out between the two groups. Investigations by the RCAF demonstrated that the conflicts were premeditated and serious: " two home-made 'blackjacks' [clubs] were found the next day . . . and the next day, two more and a sawed-off baseball bat were found in one of the city motor buses which carried both service personnel and civilians. Up to the time of leaving Moose Jaw, neither the origin or the ownership of these had been established by the police."[14]

The fighting came to a climax on September 12, when 350 airmen came to the city for a dance at the Temple Gardens. As the dance was taking place, a small number of airmen were walking through Moose Jaw's Crescent Park where they met a group of approximately fifty youths "and were subjected to a beating," but, "fortunately without any serious injuries being sustained."[15] When news of this event reached the dance hall, two hundred airmen left the Temple Gardens and paraded the streets, searching for the assailants of their companions. Soon, large crowds gathered on Main Street. Fights broke out in several different areas of the city, but were quickly subdued by the city police. Later, RAF authorities ordered their personnel back to the station.[16] In the city, four youths were charged with "taking part in the affray." All those who were charged with participating in the event were local boys between the ages of sixteen and eighteen.[17]

The next evening, Royal Air Force men

arrived in town wearing gloves even though it was a warm evening. They were "jostling local citizens and let[ting] it be known generally they were looking for trouble". The city police reported that among the arrivals that evening was "an Air Force truck [which] came to a stop at the North side of Manitoba Street West, [and] about twenty-five Air Force Officers got out and proceeded North on the West side of Main Street taking the whole sidewalk. Pedestrians (civilians) were crowded off the curb and on to the road and also crowded into doorways. The Officers refused to make room for anyone else on the sidewalk until they reached River Street."[18] As the airmen continued, their actions "were not curbed in any way by the Service Police as far as could be observed and the Service Police, according to members of the City Police, refused to render assistance in breaking up crowds on street corners."[19] Another city police report stated: "In front of the National Cafe the group was made up of officers, warrant officers, sergeants, corporals, and other airmen and SP's . . . at that time the SP's put up as much argument as any of the other airmen, and absolutely refused to give any assistance in breaking up the crowd."[20] These groups of airmen were "accosting groups of civilian youths in a hostile manner and the general atmosphere appeared to be ominous."[21] Despite these actions, no serious incidents occurred. Most of the airmen returned to the station by midnight.

Confined to Base

On September 14, a curfew was imposed on the school by the commanding officer.[22] There was no reason in the official documents for such a long delay between the beginning of the trouble and the action on the part of George. He may not have believed the problem was as serious as it was until that day. As well, the deputy mayor of Moose Jaw made a radio broadcast the night before to remind the residents that the RAF personnel were guests of the city.[23] That same day city authorities made a request to the Saskatchewan attorney-general for assistance. A group of RCMP constables were transferred to the city, but they stayed in the police stations to be called upon in case of trouble.[24] Added to this force were twenty-seven RCAF service police who had arrived from the Command Pool, Mossbank, and Regina. These service police began patrols, working in pairs in the downtown area until early morning. No further disturbances occurred after the placement of these police forces in the city.[25]

The RCAF investigator had an interest in minimizing the significance of the discord between the civilians and the RAF personnel. This effort was important; there was a possibility that other communities might seriously question their role in supporting a local air training school. A reaction to the incidents at Moose Jaw might have taken place if there had been some suppressed tensions. The morale and discipline at other schools needed to be protected. The air force investigator described the source of the animosity as one which was caused by local youths who were "obliged to share the society of members of the fair sex around their own age, with service personnel, frequently to their disadvantage and this has apparently been the cause of frequent frictions in dance halls and such like, with the interaction of remarks which were more pointed than polite."[26] In another report submitted about the same event by the RCMP, it was noted that "the enmity is not organized, and apparently has no subversive foundation. For some time past, members of the RAF have monopolized local dances and allegedly have endeavored to monopolize the attention of local ladies. Over an extended period of time, this rivalry has increased and several fights have occurred in local halls and restaurants."[27]

The report submitted by the RCAF investigator also suggested that the civilians who had been involved were delinquents. They shared some of the responsibility for the violence because they were "youths between the ages of 16 and 18 years, mostly residing in the south side of the city in lower class homes. These youths are of the street-corner, loafer variety mostly and affect a unique manner of dress which causes them to be referred to frequently as 'zoot-suiters'"—a reference to a flamboyant style of suit popular among young men of the period, the trousers had tight cuffs, a long coat with wide lapels and large padded shoulders.[28]

The RAF blamed the violence on "aliens." The youths may have been "loafers," but they certainly were not aliens, and they had been provoked.[29] Not only had the RAF personnel monopolized the dances, they had been reported to have pushed and shoved local youths while questioning them about their patriotism. The result was fights in dances and restaurants.[30] Had the disturbances continued, they would have become much more violent. The airmen would have had to contend with the adults of the city. It was made clear that "'local adult citizens were going to join in the affray unless the RAF personnel discontinued their aggressive tactics.' These same residents said 'that they would join in with the youths if the RAF didn't learn to behave themselves and that further they would from now on close their houses to members of the RAF.'"[31]

Following September 14, 1944, there were no further disturbances. The Royal Air Force liaison in Ottawa and the *Daily Diary* of the Moose Jaw service flying training school denied that there had been any problems.[32] The responses to the disturbances were described in a letter to the RCMP from H. F. Gordon, deputy minister for air, on October 21, 1944: "From a perusal of the contents of the reports, I feel, however, that no useful purpose would be served in pursuing the matter any further, particularly since there has been no indication of any continuance of the trouble and [the school] has now been disbanded. I, therefore, hope that you will agree to the conclusion of the matter."[33] As in 1943, those who appeared to be the leaders of the disturbances were courtmartialed.[34] In early November 1944, the station was closed. It is not clear if the disturbances hastened the closing of the school as there was a reduction in the size of the Training Plan occurring at the time.

Following the air school's disbanding Number Four Training Command was transferred from Calgary to Moose Jaw. After the war, a permanent RCAF base was established at the city. The disturbances of 1944, which were not remembered to the detriment of the Canadian forces, had no lasting consequences.

12

A Crisis of Its Own

The enthusiasm for the BCATP that swept the West was tempered with the stresses of the fast development of the air schools and the arrival of thousands of air crew. This enthusiasm and the ominous realization of what the huge air training facilities meant was reflected in the Rivers, Manitoba, newspaper, *The Gazette*, when it reprinted an article from the *Winnipeg Tribune* on January 30, 1941:

The Empire Training Scheme, perhaps Canada's biggest single effort in the war, provides special opportunities and imposes specially heavy responsibilities upon the West, since so many of the training schools are located here. Because of their very nature these schools have been placed far away from the major urban centres, and are, for the most part, situated in sparsely populated communities.

At Rivers, for example, the number of officers and men at the air navigation school far exceeds the population of the nearby town. At Carberry, the number of British RAF men at the service flying training school already about equals the entire population and will shortly outnumber it heavily—roughly 1,100 to 760. The people of Rivers and Carberry are doing a real job to provide hospitality for the RAF and RCAF alike. But their facilities are limited and they need help.

The various auxiliary services are doing a great job. For example, the YMCA maintains full-time secretaries at Rivers, Carberry, and Brandon, in addition to providing much equipment and facilities.

A serious responsibility lies [on] the West to do its very utmost in acting as host to these thousands of young men who are being trained to fight our battle, and whom, for the most part, we never see because they are stationed at isolated points.[1]

Too Many Jobs!

The huge construction projects at new airports called for labourers and tradesmen in numbers not thought possible in the Prairies before the war. Labour shortages first affected the construction sites, then struck every area of production, affecting the service industries and even the annual harvests everywhere.

High employment quickly became noted in the press as the construction continued. On November 20, 1940, Virden's *Empire-Advance* published a report about the local construction: "The Bird Construction Company Ltd. has the contract and under the direction of Mr. Sutherland, their representative here, work is progressing as fast as delivery of material will permit." The report continued: "Cement is being poured for the substantial foundations on which the larger hangars will be erected. Lumber is arriving at the rate of three or more carloads a day and very soon a larger number of workmen can be employed. There does not appear to be any scarcity of men. A trip to the airport Monday morning found about fifty men working and a hundred more on the ground looking for jobs."[2] It was not long before the extra hundred men had employment.

The following year, the *Weyburn Review* reported: "High speed was the great factor in construction. . . . But the speed is determined by the number of men it is possible to hire. There was a day when real tradesmen were plentiful . . . but if there ever was a surplus it has disappeared. As the months roll by the labour situation gets more and more acute and if we were to have another building campaign on the Prairies like this fall construction companies would find it more difficult to get sufficient help. Delivery of material is also becoming more serious as the days go by."[3]

Once the construction was complete, many jobs were created at the schools. A typical report was published in *The Neepawa Press*: "Number 35 EFTS operated by the Miramichi company, increased its size by one third in July . . . the civilian operators have employed approximately two hundred men and women from the district."[4]

The first members of the Women's Division arrive at the train station at Claresholm, Alberta on February 23, 1942. (PL 6974)

On Anzac Day, April 25, 1944, the men in blue parade in the small prairie community of Portage la Prairie. (PAM, Gingras, Charles J. 73)

Work is being rushed to construct hangars at the bombing and gunnery school at Mossbank, Saskatchewan. Contractors had to use every piece of equipment they had, including horse-drawn wagons, to move soil. (PL 1669)

More Help Wanted

Employment levels remained high throughout the war years. At the same time, the population of the Prairies was decreasing. The population of Saskatchewan, then the most populated of the prairie provinces, dropped by more than 61,000 between 1939 and 1941. The drop of population in Alberta and Manitoba was less dramatic; Manitoba's population dropped by about 4,500 and Alberta's only by about 600. The population continued to drop as the war continued.[5]

The number of people on relief also dropped, partly because of the high number of western Canadian men and women who enlisted and migrated to other provinces. As well, there was an economic recovery in the West in 1938 and crops had been good. As a result, the cost of relief began to fall and continued to decline during the years preceding the war. The Saskatoon *Star Phoenix* reported in the autumn of 1940 that the costs of relief had dropped substantially: "From the peak year of 1937–38 when Saskatchewan was staggering under its heaviest burden of direct relief and agricultural aid, the province has shown a marked improvement and relief this year . . . the contributing factors to the improved relief conditions are good crop conditions last year, good crop conditions this year, which resulted in no agricultural aid problem for feed and seed, and increased employment due to war industries and for enlistments."[6] In addition, the Swift Current *Sun* reported, the "average annual wage rate for male farm help in 1941 was $352 compared with $275 in 1940."[7]

Back to the Farm

As the fall of 1942 approached, it became clear that there was a shortage of farm labour. Public appeals were made across the Prairies. The *Assiniboia Times* called on high school students to consider helping in the harvest as their "patriotic duty to assist in harvesting."[8] The *Selkirk Record* reported that "the Manitoba crop is coming on well and it is vitally important that it should be safely harvested, since this province is anxious to play its full part in producing the food supply so vitally needed for the fighting forces as well as Canada's civic population." At the same time, it was "estimated that approximately 250,000 workers have left Canadian farms to join our fighting forces and engaged in war industries. The drain on farm help continues. If Manitoba farm crops are to be harvested, help must be made available."[9]

As well, the Rivers *Gazette* reported, "Many of our young men are in uniform, and while there is a move to get military men released for harvest duties, it may still be quite a job to provide the necessary seasonal help. We recall that the last war, the problem [was] partially solved by groups of men going out from town to nearby farms, and stooking for two or three hours in the evening. A couple of carloads, say ten men, can make quite a change in the appearance of a field in a brief time."[10]

When it was obvious that there was an acute shortage of farm labour, the response from the air force was not delayed. The Swift Current *Sun*, in an article entitled: "Response From The Air Force Has Been Gratifying," reported: "About 50 English airmen have come to the national selective service office and offered to go on the farms. The majority of the men had only 48-hour leave. The secretary was able to place four of these lads who are on 7-day leave, but expected to place more. No men on short leaves have been placed as yet."[11]

Although the service of the airmen remained on a volunteer basis, there was no lack of it. This was the case in Alberta, where the *Edmonton Journal* reported: "There is no lack of harvest help this year, and the chief worry of employment officials is trying to get all the applicants placed. . . . We have been sending out about 60 men a day for the past week, and we have more applicants than there are jobs. . . . The same situation existed in Medicine Hat and Lethbridge . . . [A] report from Calgary said the employment bureau there was able to fill all orders for help, although there was no apparent surplus of men."[12]

Members of the Dauphin service flying training school help with the haying. With the loss of so many local residents to the services and war industries, farmers across the Prairies turned to the local schools to assist with the harvest. (FPA 128138357)

One trainee, Phil Ellison, recalling the help airmen gave to farmers across the West, said, "I think it was good fun. The boys had a hell of a time going out—they had never seen a farm, never seen wheat, and were out stooking, throwing a few bundles, because there were still a lot of threshing outfits at that time."[13]

Good Times Again

Economic recovery also came to the service industries in the host communities. With the coming of the new air training schools, some businesses that had closed down during the Depression reopened. Bus and taxi firms, drug stores, shoe repair shops, restaurants, beer parlours, movie houses, hotels, dance halls, clothing stores, laundries, barber shops, and even the churches benefited from the coming of the air training schools. One employee of the transportation company in Moose Jaw, Bill Hemstreet, remembered that the taxi firms in the city recovered to such an extent that they decided:

To help the 'War Effort' . . . and decided to charge one dollar for a trip to or from the airport . . . This would take up to a half hour and the drivers could make more money driving within the city. Therefore, there was always a friendly competition between the various drivers to see who could make the round trip the fastest. . . . When any fellows from Caron missed the bus, we had to get permission from [the] RCMP to go more than twenty miles outside the city. Sometimes we even had a trip to Mossbank.

The taxi companies in Moose Jaw were not the only business to gain extra revenue from the Air Training Plan. Hemstreet went on to say that "the Moose Jaw Transportation Co. found a bunch of old buses and ran regular service to [the Moose Jaw school and the school] at Caron. The [Moose Jaw] run was quite frequent, as they carried civilian workers back and forth, as well as a steady flow of airmen."[14]

The good business that the airmen brought to the local service industries was also remembered in Assiniboia. A retrospective article in the Assiniboia's *Times* in 1985 mentioned that the bus that brought airmen and civilians to and from the base "stopped near the Dove Cafe, corner of North Main and Railroad. . . . The White Dove was run by Greeks and did a great business at this time, serving many grilled cheese sandwiches and hot chocolate as we waited for the bus. Mostly officers stopped here while the trainees patronized the Club Cafe across the street."[15]

However, the growth was restricted to recovering to pre-Depression levels and not beyond because of wartime restrictions on materials and the limited supply of labourers.

Ken Melby, an airframe tradesman, remembered that the labour shortage was severe: "In my own case, I worked most of the time at nights, therefore I was free during the days. They were so short of people to work in town, that I worked in a grocery store several hours a day and on my days off. People were scarce. Everybody was in the services that could be."[16]

Local businesses had to supply the air schools with essential products. As one airman, who instructed at Dauphin, Manitoba, recalled, "Even farmers were selling fresh products to the stations."[17]

Controlling the Growth

Because of the stresses that the war placed on the economy and the uncertainty over how long it would last, the federal government quickly implemented strict controls over the economy. Everything was regulated and restricted in some form, but the war effort in general and not the BCATP had brought about these restrictions.

One case of wartime restrictions reported in the Virden newspaper, *The Empire-Advance*, was the limits restaurants had to accept on the prices they set: "All menus served and maximum prices for all meals, lunches and refreshments must be filed with the Wartime Prices and Trade Board by any person starting a new restaurant or buying one already in operation. [As well] Prices charged in a new restaurant which includes hotel dining room, lunch counter or hot dog stand, must be no higher than those charged by competitors in the same class in the same locality. If there are no competitors in the same class the prices will be set by the Services Administration of the Board."[18]

One ground crew tradesman, A. S. Edger, recalled, "There was more money, but they froze wages. If we were working for a hundred dollars a month in 1940, [we] worked for a hundred dollars a month until 1945, if you stayed at the same job. There was no chance of a raise unless you were promoted. The same was for cost. The prices were frozen on everything."[19] Phil Ellison remembered that "there were jobs and things were sure better than they had been before."[20] A flying instructor at Yorkton, Ken Currie, captured the sentiment of the time when he remembered that "people realized that there was a war on and we had to pull together. You learned to live with less—sugar was rationed, as was gasoline and tires."[21]

Women's Division members at dinner in the mess at Claresholm, Alberta. (PL 6977)

A Place to Stay?

The coming of the air training schools also created a housing crisis. On the Prairies, the huge influx of airmen and their families created a need for rental accommodations. At the same time, there was a housing shortage because of the war restraints on building materials. Very few host communities were without a housing shortage during the war. Even though trainees remained on the stations in barracks, permanent staff often lived in the nearby towns and cities.

Ken Currie recalled the housing situation at Yorkton: "Living accommodation came at a premium. You got what you could and hung onto it. We were thankful when people opened their homes to us. This place where we stayed was owned by a widow. It was a big house—she had two rooms upstairs, opposite to each other and we shared the bathroom. In winter time, it was usually quite cold and we cooked with a coal oil stove which we had to keep on to heat the place."[22]

One of the only locations to have a very limited housing problem was Saskatoon, the location of Number Four Service Flying Training School and Number Seven Initial Training School. The Saskatoon *Star Phoenix* reported on September 5, 1940, that "the opening of the Saskatoon school should have little effect on the rents in this city. It was learned that the central personnel of the school will be required to live in barracks at the airdrome and that the bringing of families to the city or living out of the barracks will not be encouraged."[23]

Saskatoon was the exception. Cities as large as Edmonton, Calgary, Regina, and Winnipeg experienced difficulties. The *Calgary Herald* pointed out "Nearly every city in Canada is enjoying what might be described as a war boom. People are moving in; new industries are being started up. And as all this goes on, the housing problem in Canadian cities becomes acute. In many cities of Canada, it is a problem; no more. In Calgary, it is a tragedy. . . . The situation is generally bad across Canada today, with Calgary, Edmonton, and Lethbridge the worst situated of any Canadian city. At Ottawa, Kingston, and Barrie, rents have been booming upwards, and home construction is being rushed."[24]

The city that had one of the most critical housing situations was Winnipeg. In 1941, the *Winnipeg Tribune* reported, "For several years [the] chief inspector of sanitation and housing has been pointing to a housing situation in Winnipeg which was rapidly growing worse. His report for 1940 reveals a situation which has now become critical." The *Tribune* continued:

In 1940, states the report, 307 new dwellings were built and 30 were demolished, leaving a net gain of only 277 dwellings. There was also an increase of 116 in the number of suites. But against these very low figures there were no less than 4,658 marriages. Assuming that only three-fourths of these marriages were of city people, the rate of housing increase would, therefore, be only one dwelling or suite for approximately every eight marriages.

At the end of 1940 there were only 157 vacant dwellings and 180 vacant suites in the city. Of the dwellings, only 139 were judged to be at all fit for human occupation. Of this number, only 33 were of five rooms or less, the type of accommodation most in demand; which means of course, that more families are being forced to crowd together in contravention of our health bylaws.

On the enforced doubling of families, Mr. Officer has much to say that is right to the point. . . . We already have in Winnipeg many of the conditions found in the slums of European cities.[25]

A. S. Edger remembered the housing problem when he was working at the airport at Winnipeg. "They built the war time houses . . . but, they had a hell of a time getting material and labour . . . immediately after the war there was a burst of building, especially in Winnipeg. When I came back to Moose Jaw, it was pretty hard to get a house here too."[26] Phil Ellison, an air gunner, recalled that "down at Mossbank there was one fella that hauled in some granaries and rented them for twenty-five dollars a month. At that time, it seemed like a big figure."[27]

In most cases, communities that hosted an air training facility had severe housing shortages. However, the smaller communities had fewer houses and therefore less space for air personnel. One case was reported by *The Estevan Mercury* in the summer of 1942 with the opening of the service flying training school in that community: "Plain ordinary hospitality is spurred by downright necessity in the matter of finding housing accommodation for the wives and families who are coming from England to Estevan in the near future. A solution must be reached if these war guests are not to discover they have traded bombs for blizzards."

The federal government was to help pay for both the building and the supply of services like sewer and water to the new wartime houses:

An urgent appeal must be made to Ottawa for advice and assistance. It is noted that the City of Sudbury has recently found itself in a similar situation, which is being overcome by a federal government building program in which permanent dwellings are being constructed rather than temporary structures which are prey to wide variations in climate such as are found here. The cost of sewer and water installations is being borne by the government but the responsibility of supervising and renting falls upon the municipality. A proportionate share of the return from renting the houses is to be worked out between the municipality and the government.

Similar assistance is badly needed in Estevan, but even if it could be obtained there would still be the question of what to do in the meantime. Accommodation will have to be provided somehow for about 25 small families within the next two or three months. It is one of the most difficult wartime assignments Estevan has yet had to undertake. Whoever assists in meeting it, either at personal inconvenience or by the investment of capital, will be performing a genuine service in the national emergency.[28]

These sentiments were echoed across the Prairies. The solution was to either build more houses or to increase the number of suites for rent. A plan reported in the *Weyburn Review* in the fall of 1942 was "of interest to great many home owners ... who have houses which are larger than they need for their own use ... a home extension plan, designed to create new housing accommodation by means of loans to owners ... is now in operation."[29] This plan provided government loans for work on homes to create new suites for rent.

One account of the housing shortage and the subsequent development of suites in houses said: "There was a big rush to erect the 'wartime' houses. Also many houses were divided into apartments, or suites. Some of these were very substandard and there was a steady stream of couples moving into and out of these places every two weeks of the month. . . . Of course

Airmen trainees at work in the wireless school, Tuxedo, Winnipeg. (FPA 128138350)

there were a good number of landlords (ladies) who truly tried to supply the best for the tenants, but riding the Depression for so many years and a lot of material now on ration to civilians, many improvements were not easy to come by."[30]

Jim Kirk, an instructor at Dauphin, remembered that "housing was always tight. Usually you got housing through the station by word of mouth. If somebody was leaving or if they knew of a vacant room they would pass word on to their friends." Kirk recalled one time when "about fifteen personnel were posted off the station to Montreal where they were due for a posting overseas. Word went around that a lot of these chaps had rooms in town and were giving them up. I happened to get a room from one of these chaps that had gone on the postings. We moved in and about ten days later the guy came walking up to me on the station and asked if there was any chance of getting his room back. I asked him, 'What are you doing back here? I thought you were on a posting.' He said, 'We got to Montreal and they didn't know anything about it.' The whole thing came up over a rumour of some sort."[31]

Another solution that was found in Yorkton, Swift Current, and Claresholm, was to rent out tourist cabins. As fall approached in 1942, the families of the airmen living in the cabins requested that the cabins be winterized so that they could continue living in them through the winter months. Swift Current turned down the request, but *The Yorkton Enterprise* reported: "As a result of the decision of the Auto Camp Committee of Yorkton and District Board of Trade to winterize the cabins in the camp on Laurier Avenue, accommodation for approximately 15 families will be made possible. . . . The cost to make the change was small and that the rent coming from the families of airmen now residing in these cabins will soon pay for the necessary outlay."[32] Both Swift Current and Yorkton, like all the major centres in the West, continued to seek help from the federal government for loans to construct needed houses. These loans were approved late in the autumn of 1942. As winter approached, there was a rush of building. Although the housing problem was not completely solved, it was eased considerably.[33]

Boomtown Springs Up

Another solution to the housing shortage, reported at the remote Dafoe bombing and gunnery school, was a temporary village formed across the road from the station. The *Daily Diary* reported on August 12, 1942, "Passengers on this aircraft [that had arrived] from Saskatoon were [the] Rental Administrators of Canada, and [the] representative for the Western Provinces on the War Time Prices and Trade Board. These gentlemen paid a visit to 'Boom Town' the mushroom village that has sprung up across the road from the Station, and where it has been felt the situation presented a considerable problem to Service personnel who wished to have their families living near the Station. After looking the situation over, [the visitors decided] urgent action is necessary in the matter."[34] No further mention of "Boom Town" was made in the *Diary*. Another account of the Dafoe bombing and gunnery school's "boom town" stated: "A small village known locally as 'Boomtown' had mushroomed outside the station gates, and the cafe there vied with the station YMCA as the social centre for the station personnel. I think there were about ten business premises of one sort or another in Boomtown."[35]

Watching the Rents

As was foreseen in the local newspapers at the beginning of the war, rents for accommodation increased, especially in smaller communities which had fewer houses and rooms to rent to air personnel. The response from the government was rent controls. In Davidson, the *Leader* reported some examples of the new

Airmen who have completed their training wait at Winnipeg's Canadian Pacific Railway station prior to their departure overseas. (FPA 128138349)

controls: "A two-room light house-keeping suite renting for $35 was lowered to $27.50; two rooms in the back of a house were lowered from $30 to $20; a four roomed house rent was lowered from $35 to $22.50, and a five-roomed house from $32.50 to $22.50. . . . [the government agent for rent controls] said he found the landlords were for the most part reasonable and were willing to co-operate as far as they could to avoid a rental spiral."[36] This report of the changes in rental rates across Saskatchewan in 1943 was typical. There was little negative reaction to the rates in the local newspapers.

Although there was a great deal to be gained from the massive air training effort in the western provinces, there was a significant price to pay for it. The host communities had to make significant efforts to house the massive numbers of people who arrived. These efforts were hampered by wartime restrictions and labour shortages. Yet, in the face of the problems that existed, the communities were able to find creative and new solutions to the difficulties that came with the benefits of the Air Training Plan on the Prairies.

13

Mackenzie King, Diefenbaker, and the Struggle for a School

With the political patronage that was seen across western Canada, it was not surprising when Prime Minister Mackenzie King's riding of Prince Albert received both an elementary flying training school and an air observer school. What was extraordinary was that the air observer school never received the paved runways that it required. Because of the lack of these runways, the school was closed in 1942. King found himself powerless, at the late stage he intervened, to change the decision.

Mackenzie King had been representing Prince Albert since shortly after the 1925 federal election, when the Liberal party had been returned to office but King suffered a personal defeat in the North York constituency. The Liberal member of Parliament for Prince Albert, Charles Macdonald, stepped aside to allow King to be elected in a by-election.

Air observer schools, like elementary flying training schools, were operated by civilian companies. Often, the air observer schools were established at the same airports as elementary schools. Prince Albert was not an exception when, in 1940, it won the right to operate Number Six Air Observer School together with Number Six Elementary Flying School. The elementary school, which was run by a joint venture of the flying clubs of Prince Albert and Saskatoon, opened on July 22, 1940. The observer school was to open in September. While the hangars and other buildings needed for the air observer school were under construction, a search was underway for a civilian company to operate it. There was a great deal of support among city leaders for a local company, M. and C. Aviation, to win the contract.

Keeping It Local

The company had been operated for nearly ten years by Richard Mayson, a fighter pilot in the Great War, and Angus Campbell, an engineer and one of Mayson's pupils from the Saskatoon Flying Club. The two men formed M. and C. Aviation which offered scheduled flights to northern destinations such as Fond du Lac, Ile a la Crosse, and Yellowknife. They also fought fires and flew emergency flights when required. The company had been successful in its northern service even with competition from the largest air transport company in Canada, Canadian Airways, which provided service to the north as well.[1]

However, the air observer schools required administrative abilities and facilities of a larger airline. M. and C. had only five aircraft compared to thirty-five aircraft of Canadian Airways. Another competitor was the larger Prairie Airways of Moose Jaw. At the same time, M. and C. was busy with a contract to operate a repair depot for the de Havilland Tiger Moths used by Number Six Elementary Flying Training School.[2]

For these reasons, the authorities in Ottawa were actively looking to companies like Canadian Airways. It was strongly rumoured in May 1940 that the contract would be given to Yukon Southern Air Transport, a company owned and operated by Grant McConnachie of Edmonton. This possibility was strongly opposed by Mayson and Campbell and the business community of Prince Albert, which believed the school should be operated by the local company. The city council and the board of trade wrote letters to the prime minister while Mayson and Prince Albert's mayor travelled to Ottawa to put pressure on their member of Parliament, Prime Minister King, to win the observer school for M. and C. Aviation. The effectiveness of this lobbying was seen when a letter from the Prime Minister's Office to the secretary of the RCAF noted that: "Mr. Henry of the Prime Minister's Office has drawn my attention to the fact that information has been received from Prince Albert to the effect that Number Six Air Observer School Prince Albert, is likely to be operated by a company with headquarters at Edmonton (McConnachie?) whereas the M. & C. Company and Canadian Airways are already located at Prince Albert." The letter concluded that, "It is noted that the McConnachie Co. is extra provincial and that the public interest would be better served by having the contract in the hands of local companies preferred, or at least a company of [the] Province of Saskatchewan origin."[3]

At the same time, the competition was

Tiger Moths lined up outside the hangers at Prince Albert, where there were no paved runways. (RA 9616[1])

being drawn away by other wartime contracts. The central competitor, McConnachie, received an offer to work on the North-West Staging Route with the American Army Air Corps. Canadian Airways won a contract to operate Number Two Air Observer School at Edmonton. The last competitor, Prairie Airways, based in Moose Jaw, was given the contract to operate Number Three Air Observer School in Regina. Therefore, the only company left to operate the air observer school was M. and C.[4]

Mayson and Campbell were given the contract to operate the Air Observer School after they reorganized their company as a Crown corporation and provided fifty thousand dollars capital. Because of the lobbying that had been carried out, relations between the new observer school and the training command administering the schools in northern Saskatchewan were strained. Those in the Winnipeg training command headquarters who had been against a small company operating the observer school had been overruled.

The ill feeling was clear in a memorandum written to defend the school's management in June 1942:

We have had happy relations with all officers of the RCAF Supervisory staff at our school, and also with those of No. 2 Training Command with the exception of Air Officer Commanding, Air Commodore Shearer. He has never even been pleased, and has made his dislike of us evident in many ways. In fifteen months of operations he has visited us only twice—once on the occasion of the Prime Minister's visit and the other time on the official visit of the Inspector General. It is most difficult to get an interview with him to discuss the school's business. On the occasion of his meeting with the Prime Minister interview with the AOC, here he was jumped on and very rudely dealt with.[5]

It was this animosity between training command and the air observer school that brought about many of the problems that led to its closing.[6]

One Too Many Schools for Prince Albert?

Early in 1942, the RCAF was considering the expansion of the Air Training Plan. Because the war effort required more navigators, existing schools were being prepared for expansions and, where necessary, observer schools were being separated from elementary flying schools. In June, it was announced that the observer school at Prince Albert, like many of the others, was to be expanded. But this decision was not final; the decision to close the school was quickly announced.

To justify closing the observer school, the RCAF pointed out that it had lost flying time because of wet weather in spring. This loss of flying time was obviously caused by the absence of hard-surfaced runways at the school, the only observer school without them. Although it was possible to fly the small Tiger Moths used at the elementary flying school off sod fields, it was more difficult to fly the larger two-engine Ansons required for the observers. Mayson argued, "Poor aircraft serviceability has nothing to do with the difference in flying hours. Our shortage of flying hours in April is solely due to lack of hard-surfaced runways, melting snows and a muddy field. We are handicapped, because after melting snows and rains, we have to wait anywhere from half a day to three weeks for the aerodrome to dry before we can use it, and the consequent shortage of flying hours, which under such circumstances we can do nothing about."[7] It was almost impossible to get airplanes off the muddy field. When heavy aircraft like the Anson used such a soft field, they broke down more often.[8]

Mayson put the blame for the lack of hard-surfaced runways directly at the door of the commanding officer of training command, Air Commodore Shearer. It is difficult to determine who made the decision not to construct hard-surfaced runways at Prince Albert but it was routine to have them built at all schools. There should have been no question that an aviation centre as important as Prince Albert, with two schools, should have had hard-surfaced runways. In a meeting of the Aerodrome Development Committee, the organization which supervised all airport construction of the Air Training Plan, on May 5, 1942, the lack of paved runways at Prince Albert was discussed. It was pointed out that the construction of the runways was delayed due to confusion over the direction of the prevailing winds at the airport site. Because the sod field appeared to be adequate at that time, nothing was done.

Mayson, thinking the decision not to pave the runways may have been related to his management, said he was prepared to resign if that would keep the air observer school in Prince Albert. The suggestion, however, made no difference to those who made the decision.[9]

The Political Dimension

Another political element was added to the picture when the intention of opening an air observer school at the village of Davidson, Saskatchewan, a part of the federal constituency of Lake Centre, was also announced. Lake Centre was represented in Parliament by John G. Diefenbaker, a well-known Progressive Conservative lawyer who lived in Prince Albert and had run against King unsuccessfully in the election of 1926. Diefenbaker, who was sitting in his first session of

Prime Minister Mackenzie King inspects troops at the Tuxedo wireless school at Winnipeg. (FPA 128138352)

Parliament, had become a loud critic of the way the contracts had been granted to construct the facilities of the Air Training Plan. He had also targeted the allowances granted to the observer and elementary flying schools as being too high. He argued that too many businessmen were benefitting from the war effort. Added to these criticisms in Ottawa, Diefenbaker had travelled to Prince Albert, where he had criticized Mayson's management of the observer school. Diefenbaker's criticisms brought about much concern in Prince Albert.[10]

With the concerns of the war, King did not have time to pay close attention to what had happened at Prince Albert until he was visited by Mayson and Mr. Sanderson, the president of the observer school, in Ottawa on June 18, 1942. That night, King recorded in his diary that "Some time was taken up tonight discussing . . . the question of the Air Training School. It is hard to tell the right and the wrong of the situation."[11] Following this, King wrote to C. G. Power, chairman of the air council, on June 23:

> *The management does not deny that operating costs are high or that flying time is too low. They contend that both these circumstances result from a single cause, namely, that the Prince Albert Air Observer School is the only school without hard-surfaced runways. . . . It is further contended by the management of the school that the development of hard-surfaced runways which would have eliminated both of these difficulties has been consistently obstructed by responsible officers who have given no good reason for such obstruction. . . .*
>
> *I understand that the training of observers is to be transferred to a large new air observer school to be located at Davidson, Saskatchewan. I am further informed that this new school is to be equipped with hard-surfaced runways. I think you will readily agree that the unwillingness to construct such runways at the existing school at Prince Albert and the readiness to construct them at Davidson demands some explanation. This is particularly true when it is realized that Prince Albert is a large community which is a natural focus of civilian flying whereas Davidson is a mere village. . . . It is something of a coincidence that the Air Observer School at Prince Albert should be closed at the very time a large school is opened in the constituency of a member [Diefenbaker] who, during the present session, has shown particular zeal in his criticism of the organization of air observer schools.*[12]

Power had already made the decision to double the size of the elementary flying school at Prince Albert as well as to disband the city's observer school. His difficult position was made worse because he had instituted guidelines that King himself had set down: no favours were to be given to anyone as a result of political patronage, (at least the appearance of patronage was to be avoided). Yet, King was now asking Power to act on a request that was very close to political patronage. In his reply, Power pointed out that when the Air Training Plan was established it was considered more economical to put the elementary flying training schools and the observer schools together. But, because no paved runways existed at that point at Prince Albert, and none would have to be constructed if the observer school was closed, the economics of the situation had changed. He also cited another problem: "The traffic control is further aggravated by the fact that the exercises at the Elementary Schools are totally different from those at the Air Observer Schools. . . . On the other hand, when the problem of eliminating one of them arose, [we] felt the proper procedure was to eliminate the least efficient, judged by the above standards."[13]

Failure Against His Own Bureaucracy

Mackenzie King replied with a letter that made it obvious he was disappointed and irritated with his inability to change the situation. King wrote: "I do not feel that I would be justified in permitting the matter to rest at this stage. May I draw your attention to the fact that all of the points raised have been completely ignored in your reply. . . . It seems to me that there is nothing in your letter to support the decision to establish the observer school at Davidson while leaving the elementary school at Prince Albert which could not equally be urged in support of the reverse arrangement."[14]

In a letter of July 7, 1942, Power detailed each point that was taken into consideration when the decision was made to close the air observer school. He wrote that the flying hours had been lower than at other schools. Although this was caused by the fact that there was no hard-surfaced runways, again there was no explanation as to why the school had not received them. As the elementary school could continue without the construction of paved runways, he wrote, the decision would not be reversed.[15]

It was not until July 23 that King was able to reply to this letter because both King and Power were preoccupied with the important debate in the House of Commons over conscription in which the famous formula of "conscription if necessary but not necessarily conscription" was coined.[16]

In his reply, King wrote: "You point out that the operational costs at Prince Albert have been high and the flying time poor. This was [because] . . . no hard-surfaced runways were provided. . . . I would also like to know what consideration was given to the point in my letter that all other things being equal, a community of the size of Prince Albert should be given the benefit of permanent aerodrome installations rather than a small village the size of Davidson."[17]

J. L. Apedaile, the financial adviser for civilian schools, was asked by Power to prepare a reply to King's letter. The letter he prepared simply indicated once again the reasons for closing the school, and was initialled "C. G. P." King realized he was losing the battle.[18] More importantly, the war effort required more of his time. He left the issue behind with a letter that blamed the whole problem on the fact that the school had no paved runways and concluded: "I would not be doing myself or the constituency of Prince Albert justice if I did not say that, with the failure to reply to the management on this point, it will be difficult

Tiger Moths from the elementary flying school at Prince Albert early on a cold morning at Emma Lake. (PMR 81–143)

to have the people of Prince Albert believe that there has been complete fairness in the matter and that a governing motive on the part of some official has not been a desire to appease one of the chief critics of the RCAF in its Air Observer School policy."[19]

Number Six Air Observer School was officially closed in September 1942, after eighteen months of training and the graduation of 615 navigators from several different countries. With the closing, Number Six Elementary Flying Training School was doubled in size. The school continued to operate until July 1944 when the British Commonwealth Air Training Plan was reduced substantially. The elementary school had trained 2,647 pilots by that time.[20]

Mayson and Campbell continued to manage the repair depot for the elementary school until it closed. With the closure of the school, M. and C. turned to civilian commercial service with the surplus Anson Aircraft until 1947 when it was purchased by the newly formed Saskatchewan Government Airways.[21]

Davidson received an air school, but not the air observer school that King had objected to. It was a less prestigious elementary flying school. Awarding an air observer school to Davidson would have been too much of a personal humiliation for the prime minister.[22]

As large as the issue of the observer school appeared to be, the Prince Albert *Herald* had no comment about its closing because its attention was turned to the dark events of war. Germany had successfully occupied France, appeared to have the upper hand in northern Africa, and repulsed the Allies at Dieppe. The German army had begun to threaten Stalingrad as the observer school closed in September.

After the Prince Albert air observer school closed, King did not return to the constituency until the 1945 election. He may not have been surprised when he lost the constituency by 129 votes, but he must have been disappointed. However, King had no trouble finding a safe seat in Glengarry, Ontario, in order to lead his new postwar Liberal government.[23]

14

The Plan's Aviation Legacy

As the war drew to an end, fewer aircrew were required. The result was the closing of air training schools as the BCATP curtailed operations. With the closing of the school at Estevan and the transfer of the personnel, the *Estevan Mercury* published a farewell article in February 1944:

. . . as friends bid adieu to some 460 members of the RAF who left on a special train at 8:10 from the CNR depot, Estevan, on the first lap of the journey that will eventually take them home to the United Kingdom. The night was cold and shivering couples and groups stood in the dimness saying their good byes in the hope that peace-time would bring reunions. . . . As each transport arrived the men were handed a gift of cigarettes, fruit and a copy of "The Mercury" which officially bid them farewell with many messages expressing regret at their departure. Mayor H. Nicholson and H. A. Westergaard canvassed the town to raise the necessary funds to pay for the gifts which were handed out by a ladies' committee. In addition, magazines were placed on the train.

The Estevan Band under the direction of Bandmaster Johnston played in the depot waiting room, extreme cold preventing it from performing outside. Extra lights had been strung along to help illuminate the long string of fourteen cars which made up the train. On the outside of the centre was stretched a long streamer with the words 'Bundles for Britain (priority).'

In spite of the extreme cold a crowd estimated at 500 thronged the full length of the train, and with cars honking, good-byes being shouted and people waving, the train pulled out into the darkness with its tail lights gradually dimming until they had disappeared in the murk of the RAF.[1]

The fact that there was much enthusiasm among the civilian population for the airmen and airwomen who were leaving demonstrated that there was generally good relations between the air stations and the nearby communities. The warm relations resulted from a patriotic sentiment and a feeling of good will among British, Australian, New Zealand, Indian, Free French, Czechoslovakian, Norwegian, Polish, Belgian, Dutch, and Canadian airmen as well as the local residents.

Yet, newspapers across the West showed no signs of grieving at the closing of the schools. The reaction was to look to the future and make plans to consolidate the gains made during the war. Many of the air training facilities were to be reconstructed for civilian use. The *North Battleford Optimist* published a typical report about the local airport and its promising future if the population did not become complacent:

By indifference to its great importance it can peter out into a mere subsidiary of the transcontinental airlines which will crisscross the country. By concerted and aggressive action it can not only be incorporated into the national and international air services but it can be developed into a primary base for northern air routes which are at present in their infancy.

What aviation has achieved in this war is something barely understood by the general public. Improved types of airplanes, radar control, radio beams, and broadened meteorological services spanning wide areas and distances, are but a few of the wonderful developments of the past few years.

Some idea of these scientific improvements can be gained from one reference—Atlantic crossings. Before the war, the Atlantic was never flown during winter. Now crossings which began in 1940 are only part of a vast Atlantic service of a routine character, carrying passengers, mail and cargo. By May, 1944, 15,000 trans-Atlantic crossings had been made with the loss of under half of one percent, and that in spite of an enforced radio silence to avoid interception by the enemy.[2]

Although this was a common overstatement, the airports in many communities *were* used after the war. Even though the numbers of aircraft in the skies of the Prairies decreased dramatically, the main airfields became important for civilian purposes. Some of these airports acted as links in transcontinental air travel as it spread across the country immediately after the war. Later, when jet aircraft services were established, the importance of the many smaller air links was lost.[3]

The New Industry of the Air

In the West, there was respect for air travel before the war because aircraft serviced isolated communities across the Prairies and in the North. Many cities and

The final parade in 1945 brings to a close the BCATP at Portage la Prairie. (PAM, Gingras, Charles J. 105)

towns had benefited from carriers like Canadian Airlines, Athabaska Airlines, and Prairie Airways. Even the smaller companies such as M. and C. of Prince Albert had played a role in aviation.

An important outcome of the war was the creation of Canadian Pacific Airways from ten smaller companies that had managed the air observer schools in 1942. The largest national airline, Trans-Canada Airlines (TCA) also had expanded as a result of the war. The number of passengers travelling on TCA had increased substantially. In 1939, the airline carried 21,569 passengers. This figure increased in 1945 to 183,121. This kind of increase was seen in the number of miles flown, with three million miles flown in 1939 and over 11.5 million in 1945. In the same period, the number of employees increased from 497 to 3,272. In addition, there was vigorous competition to establish routine flights in the Pacific. Domestically, Wardair was founded in 1946.[4]

In the postwar era, the exploitation of natural resources in western Canada helped to continue the economic growth that had begun in 1938, but it was the achievement of the Air Training Plan that brought about the maturity of the region.

End of Alienation

The British Commonwealth Air Training Plan gave the western provinces many new facilities and a new confidence. It was, in fact, the contribution that the West made to the national war effort through the Plan that ushered in a new era of declining western alienation. Western alienation was an expressed feeling of being isolated from and exploited by the rest of the nation. This led to a sense of helplessness across the Prairies during the Depression. With the important contribution it had made to the Air Training Plan and its improved economy, the West no longer felt helpless. The Prairies had won a position in the Plan equal to that of any other region. It came out of the Second World War as an equal partner in Canada, a position it had been calling for since Confederation.

A Canadian Pacific Airlines aircraft is loaded in September 1949. (NMST 5583)

Further, the very nature of the British Commonwealth Air Training Plan brought the Prairies out of its isolation. With the arrival of the trainees from many parts of Canada and from many different countries, residents of the western provinces were made more aware of the world around them. At the same time, the development of airports across the region brought improved air transportation. The airplanes were more effective than the trains the Prairies had previously depended on. Ottawa, which had been days away only a few years earlier, was now only hours away.

With an end to the isolation of the Prairies and the new confidence that the British Commonwealth Air Training Plan had brought, the West was now far from the state of alienation it had been in before the war.

Notes

Photographic Note

The photographs that are contained in this book have been supplied by a number of different institutions and each has abbreviations to identify them. The Department of National Defence photographs have either PL or PMR to identify them. The Glenbow Museum photographs are identified with NA, while the Western Canada Pictorial Index photos have JRA, FPA, or ABA at the beginning of the number. The Saskatchewan Archives Board are numbered with RA or RB. As well, the Provincial Archives of Manitoba will be identified with PAM, while the National Museum of Science and Technology are given the initials NMST.

Notes for Chapter 1
Canada Becomes the Centre for Training Aircrew

1 F. J. Hatch, *The Aerodrome of Democracy: Canada and the British Commonwealth Air Training Plan, 1939–1945* (Ottawa: Directorate of History, Department of National Defence, Occasional Paper No. 1, 1983), p. 1.

2 S. F. Wise, *Canadian Airmen and the First World War: The Official History of the Royal Canadian Air Force Vol. I* (Toronto: University of Toronto Press, 1981), pp. 7, 23–45.

3 *Ibid.*, pp. 119–120.

4 *Ibid.*

5 W. A. B. Douglas, *The Creation of a National Air Force: The Official History of the Royal Canadian Air Force, Vol. II* (Toronto: University of Toronto Press, 1986), pp. 35–36; F. J. Hatch, "The British Commonwealth Air Training Plan 1939–1945" (Unpublished Ph.D. dissertation, University of Ottawa, 1969), pp. 16–17.

6 Hatch, *The Aerodrome of Democracy*, p. 7.

7 *Ibid.*, p. 8; Canada, *Documents on Canadian External Relations, Vol. 6, 1936–1939* (hereafter *DCER*), (Ottawa: Queen's Printer, 1972), p. 208. Memorandum by the Prime Minister to O. D. Skelton.

8 Canada, House of Commons, *Debates*, July, 1, 1938, cols. 4523–4532. See also, Douglas, *The Creation of a National Air Force*, p. 194.

9 *DCER, Vol. 6, 1936–1939*, p. 218. British High Commissioner to Prime Minister, July 7, 1938.

10 The United Kingdom, House of Commons, *Debates*, July 7, 1938, Col. 595.

11 *DCER, Vol. 6, 1936–1939*, p. 225. Prime Minister to British High Commissioner, September 6, 1938, pp. 225, 227–230. British High Commissioner to Prime Minister, December 9, 1938, and Memorandum by British Government, December 9, 1938, pp. 227–230.

12 *Ibid.*, pp. 230–232. Prime Minister to British High Commissioner, December 31, 1938.

13 *Public Archives of Canada*, Records of the RCAF, Record Group (hereafter RG) 24, Volume 3531, file HQ 898–6–41, "Memorandum of Agreement: Training of Short Service Commissioned Officers (General Duties Branch)." Cited in Hatch, "The BCATP 1939–1945," p. 56.

14 Hatch, *The Aerodrome of Democracy*, pp. 11–12.

15 *Ibid.*, p. 13.

16 *DCER, Vol. 7, Part I, 1939-1941*, p. 551.

17 J. W. Pickersgill, *The Mackenzie King Record, Vol I, 1939–1944* (Toronto: University of Toronto Press, 1960), p. 40.

18 *DCER, Vol. 7, Part I, 1939–1941*, pp. 552–555. Minutes of Emergency Council (*Committee on General Policy*) of Cabinet, Sept. 28, 1939.

19 Hatch, *The Aerodrome of Democracy*, p. 16.

20 *Ibid.*; *DCER, Vol. 7, Part I, 1939–1941*, pp. 580–581. Memorandum from Chairman, Air Mission of Great Britain to Prime Minister, October 13, 1939; Douglas *The Creation of a National Air Force*, pp. 209–210.

21 Douglas *The Creation of a National Air Force*, pp. 206–208; Hatch, *The Aerodrome of Democracy*, p. 16.

22 Hatch, *The Aerodrome of Democracy*, p. 17.

23 *Ibid.*; R. S. Sayers, *Financial Policy: 1939–45* (London: Longmans, Green and Company, 1956), pp. 324–333.

24 Sayers, *Financial Policy*, pp. 324–333; see also, Canada, *Agreement Relating to Training of Pilots and Aircraft Crews in Canada and Their Subsequent Service between the United Kingdom, Canada, Australia and New Zealand Signed at Ottawa, December 17, 1939*, Printed in full in C. P. Stacey, *Arms, Men and Government: The War Policies of Canada, 1939–1945*, (Ottawa: Queen's Printer, 1970), Appendix "J", pp. 565–578. (Cited as B*CATP Agreement* after this point).

25 *DCER, Vol. 7, Part I, 1939–1941*, pp. 620–621, Rogers to Balfour, Nov. 27, 1939.

26 *Ibid.*, pp. 635–636, Secretary of State for External Affairs to Dominions Secretary, November 28, 1939; Douglas, *The Creation of a National Air Force*, p. 212–213.

27 *DCER, Vol. 7, Part I, 1939–1941*, p. 636, Secretary of State for External Affairs to Dominions Secretary, Nov. 28, 1939; p. 637, Dominions Secretary of State for External Affairs to Dominions Secretary, Dec. 1, 1939.

28 W. L. M. King, *The British Commonwealth Air Training Plan Broadcast by Right Hon. W. L. Mackenzie King, M. P., Prime Minister of Canada, Sunday, December 17, 1939* (Ottawa: J. O. Patenaude, 1939), p. 16. The emphasis is by the author.

29 Hatch, *Aerodrome of Democracy*, p. 23.

30 Canada, *Report of the Royal Commission on Dominion–Provincial Relations*, Book I, p. 150; *Book II, Recommendations, en passim.*

Notes for Chapter 2
Preparing for the Great Undertaking

1 Douglas, *The Creation of a National Air Force*, p. 220.

2 *Ibid.*

3 *Ibid.*, pp. 121–123.

4 Hatch, *Aerodrome of Demoncracy*, p. 42; Douglas, *The Creation of a National Air Force*, pp. 123–124.

5 *Ibid.*, p. 124; R. W. Ryan, *From Boxkite to Boardroom* (Moose Jaw: Moose Jaw Publications, 1987), *en passim*

6 Hatch, *Aerodrome of Demoncracy*, p. 63.

7 *Ibid.*, pp. 63, 69–70.

8 *Ibid.*, p. 70.

9 *Ibid.*, p. 192.

Notes for Chapter 3
Building for the Future

1 The Parliament of Canada, *Sessional Papers*, and the Department of Finance publications did not contain provincial or school financial records that would allow one to estimate how much was spent in the prairie provinces reliably.

2 Hatch, *Aerodrome of Democracy*, pp. 41–42.

3 *The Edmonton Journal*, Sept. 4, 1940.

4 Interview: Don O'Hearn with the author, June 27, 1988.

5 J. W. Corman to Norman Rogers, March 18, 1940, Town Council Records, *Moose Jaw City Archives*, cited in Brereton Greenhous and Norman Hillmer, "The Impact of the British Commonwealth Air Training Plan on Western Canada: Some Saskatchewan Studies," *Journal of Canadian Studies*, Vol. 16 (Fall–Winter, 1981), p. 134.

6 Saskatoon, *Star Phoenix*, Oct. 26, 1940.

7 *Ibid.*, July 30, 1940.

8 *Souris Plaindealer*, Jan. 15, 1941.

Notes for Chapter 4
For Duty and Prosperity

1 Interview: Phil Ellison with the author, June 7, 1989.

2 Rivers, *The Gazette*, Dec. 5, 1940.

3 Virden, *Empire–Advance*, Nov. 20, 1940

4 Lethbridge, *Herald*, July 27, 1940.

5 *The Estevan Mercury*, Sept 4, 1941.

6 *Weyburn Review*, Sept. 11, 1941; Dec. 18, 1941.

7 Lethbridge, *Herald*, Sept. 18, 1940.

8 Rivers, *The Gazette*, Sept. 2, 1943.

9 Interview: J. P. Kirk with author, Sept. 29, 1987.

10 Swift Current, *The Sun*, March 14, 1944.

Notes for Chapter 5
"Cheered in the Streets"

1 *Weyburn Review*, Dec. 25, 1941; Swift Current *Sun*, June 3, 1941.
2 Letter: Dalton Deedrick to author, Oct. 14, 1986.
3 Swift Current *Sun*, June 3, 1941; letter: J.P. Kirk to author, Nov. 26, 1986; *Moose Jaw Times-Herald*, Nov. 13, 1940.
4 *The North Battleford News*, July 24, 1941.
5 *The Prairie Flyer*, March, 1944, cited in Greenhous and Hillmer, p. 139.
6 Letter: Robert Steel to the author, Sept. 3, 1986.
7 *Picton Times*, April 29, 1941, cited in Greenhous and Hilmer, p. 139.
8 Saskatoon *Star Phoenix*, Sept. 23, 1940.

Notes for Chapter 6
Going Through the Mill

1 Hatch, *Aerodrome of Democracy*, pp. 120–121; Interview: J. P. Kirk with author, Sept. 29, 1987.
2 Interview: Bill Minor with author, Oct. 3, 1987.
3 Interview: C. A. (Smoky) Robson with the author, June 7, 1989.
4 Interview: Stan Morris with the author, June 5, 1989.
5 Interview: Phil Ellison with the author, June 7, 1989.
6 Interview: Bill Minor with the author, Oct. 3, 1987.
7 Hatch, *Aerodrome of Democracy*, pp. 120–121.
8 Interview: Phil Ellison with the author, June 7, 1989.
9 Hatch, *Aerodrome of Democracy*, pp. 127–132.
10 Murray Peden, *A Thousand Shall Fall* (Stittsville, Ont.: Canada's Wings Inc., 1979), p. 16.
11 Interview: Pat Coggins with the author, June 6, 1989.
12 Interview: Stan Morris with the author, June 5, 1989.
13 Interview: Paul Heasman with the author, June 5, 1989.
14 Interview: Stan Morris with the author, June 5, 1989.
15 Interview: J. P. Kirk with author, Sept. 29, 1987.

Notes for Chapter 7
Hazards of War

1 Interview: Stan Morris with the author, June 5, 1989.
2 Swift Current *Sun*, Dec. 2, 1941.
3 *The Yorkton Enterprise*, March 13, 1941.
4 *The Neepawa Press*, Dec. 16, 1943.
5 *The Macleod Gazette*, April 10, 1941
6 Wise, p. 107.
7 *Ibid.*, pp. 103–110.
8 Hatch, *Aerodrome of Democracy*, p. 101.
9 *The Macleod Gazette*, July 30, 1942.
10 *Weyburn Review*, Aug. 6, 1942.
11 Interview: A. S. Edger with the author, Aug. 4, 1988.
12 Interview: Pat Coggins with the author, June 6, 1989.

Notes for Chapter 8
Operating the Plan

1 *The Estevan Mercury*, Feb 10, 1944.
2 Robert Collins, *The Long and the Short and the Tall* (Saskatoon: Western Producer Prairie Books, 1986), p. v.
3 Interview: J. P. Kirk with author, September 29, 1987.
4 Interview: Phil Ellison with the author, June 6, 1989.
5 *Yorkton Enterprise*, June 5, 1942.
6 *The Record of No. 7 A.O.S. R.C.A.F. Portage la Prairie, Man. 1941–1945*, p. 81.
7 Hatch, *The Aerodrome of Democracy*, p. 36.

8 *Yorkton Enterprise*, June 5, 1942.
9 *Ibid.*
10 *Ibid.*
11 *Ibid.*
12 *Ibid.*
13 Douglas, *The Creation of a National Air Force*, p. 220.
14 Interview: Don O'Hearn with the author, June 27, 1988.
15 Interview: Dorothy Currie with the author, June 8, 1989.
16 Hatch, *Aerodrome of Democracy*, p. 183.

Notes for Chapter 9
"The Tie that Binds"

1 *Yorkton Enterprise*, Dec. 2, 1941.
2 *Souris Plaindealer*, May 6, 1942.
3 *Winnipeg Tribune*, Jan. 11, 1941.
4 Dafoe No. 5 B&GS, *Diary*, Aug. 16, 1942.
5 Mossbank No. 2 B&GS, *Diary*, April 9, 1941.
6 *The Neepawa Press*, April 1, 1943.
7 Prince Albert No. 6 AOS, *Diary*, June 21, 1941; Dafoe No. 5 B&GS, *Diary*, May 16, 1942; Regina No. 15 EFTS, *Diary*, Sept. 30, 1943.
8 Claresholm, *Windy Wings*, May 1, 1943, p. 17.
9 Mossbank No. 2 B&GS, *Diary*, May 22, 1941; North Battleford No. 13 SFTS, *Diary*, Appendix "C", Dec. 1944; Dafoe No. 5 B&GS, *Diary*, Jan. 31, 1943.
10 Claresholm, *Windy Wings*, April 1, 1942, p. 11.
11 *Penhold Log*, Aug. 1944, p. 13.
12 Davidson No. 23 EFTS, *Diary*, March 16, 1944; Dafoe No. 5 B&GS, *Diary*, Feb. 2, 1942.
13 *The Neepawa Press*, April 9, 1942.
14 Davidson No. 23 EFTS, *Diary*, March 10, 1944; Mossbank No. 2 B&GS, *Diary*, Feb. 11, 1942.
15 *The Yorkton Enterprise*, Oct. 9, 1941.
16 *North Battleford Optimist*, May 6, 1943.
17 *The Estevan Mercury*, April 1, 1943.
18 *The Yorkton Enterprise*, May 1, 1941.
19 *The Winnipeg Tribune*, Jan. 25, 1941.
20 Dafoe No. 5 B&GS, *Diary*, May 1, 1941.
21 *Ibid.*
22 *Souris Plaindealer*, May 12, 1943.
23 *The Record of No. 7 A.O.S. R.C.A.F. Portage la Prairie, Man. 1941–45.*
24 Interview: Don O'Hearn with the author, June 27, 1988.
25 Letter: Dorothy Minor to the author, Feb. 26, 1987
26 Letter: Alexandria (Macdonald) Miller to Brereton Greenhous and Norman Hillmer, July 10, 1980. Copy supplied by Mrs. Miller to author.
27 Interview: Bill Minor with the author, Oct. 3, 1987.
28 North Battleford No. 13 SFTS, *Diary*, April 29, 1944.
29 Interview Dorothy and Ken Currie with the author, June 8, 1989.
30 *Final Report of the Chief of Air Staff to the Members of the Supervisory Board: British Commonwealth Air Training Plan*, April 16, 1945, p. 27.
31 Interview: Phil Ellison with the author, June 7, 1989.
32 Greenhous and Hillmer, p. 143.
33 Interview: A. S. Edger with author, Aug. 4, 1988.
34 Rivers, *The Gazette*, July 10, 1941.
35 Swift Current, *Sun* March 14, 1944.
36 *Weyburn Review*, June 18, 1942.

Notes for Chapter 10
Sharing Field and Ice

1 Saskatoon, *Star Phoenix*, July 6, 1940.
2 *The Estevan Mercury*, June 11, 1942.
3 Rivers, *The Gazette*, April 24, 1941.
4 *Souris Plaindealer*, Aug. 16, 1944.
5 Davidson No. 23 EFTS, *Diary*, Aug. 12, 1944; Mossbank No. 2 B&GS, *Diary*, Aug. 14, 1943.
6 *The Estevan Mercury*, Aug. 6, 1942.
7 Moose Jaw No. 32 SFTS, *Diary*, April 1, 1944; *The Estevan Mercury*, April 1, 1943.
8 *The Neepawa Press*, Oct. 16, 1942.
9 Rivers, *The Gazette*, Aug. 26, 1943.
10 Swift Current *Sun*, Sept. 1, 1942.
11 *The Calgary Herald*, Sept. 20, 1940.
12 Rivers, *The Gazette*, May 22, 1941.
13 *The Penhold Log*, Aug. 1944, p. 14.
14 Swift Current *Sun*, July 27, 1943.
15 Mossbank No. 2 B&GS, *Diary*, Aug. 20, 1944; Moose Jaw No. 32 SFTS, *Diary*, Aug. 31, 1944.
16 Claresholm, *Windy Wings*, April 9, 1943, p. 9.
17 *The Davidson Leader*, April 12, 1944.
18 Vince Leah, *100 Years of Hockey in Manitoba* (Winnipeg: Manitoba Hockey Player's Foundation and the Manitoba Centennial Corp., 1970), p. 39.
19 *Ibid.*, p. 40.

20 *The Yorkton Enterprise*, Feb. 1942.
21 *Ibid.*, March 6, 1942.
22 *Ibid.*, Oct. 22, 1942; Nov. 5, 1942.
23 *The Yorkton Enterprise*, Dec. 17, 1942; Dec 2, 1943.
24 Gary W. Zeman, *Alberta on Ice* (Edmonton: GMS Ventures Inc., 1985), pp. 121–122.
25 Davidson No. 23 EFTS, *Diary*, July 7, 1943, Aug. 21, 1943, July 1944, Sept. 3, 1944.
26 Swift Current *Sun*, Aug. 18, 1942.
27 *The Neepawa Press*, June 11, 1942.
28 *Estevan Mercury*, April 1, 1943.
29 Moose Jaw No. 32 SFTS, *Diary*, July 31, 1944.

Notes for Chapter 11

Zoot-Suiters and the Yellow Bellied

1 *Moose Jaw Times-Herald*, Oct. 14, 1944, p. 6; Interview: Harry Riviere with the author, Aug 4, 1987.
2 Greenhous and Hillmer, p. 140.
3 Calgary No. 4 TC, *Diary*, Appendix I, November 1940.
4 *The Prairie Flyer*, March, 1944, p. 2.
5 Calgary No. 4 TC, *Diary*, December 1941, Appendix, "Report: SFTS No. 32 Moose Jaw."
6 Interview: Fred Hawkins with the author, Aug. 4, 1987; John Wing with the author, Aug. 3, 1987; Mr. Harry Riviere with the author, Aug. 4, 1987; Roland Wilkes with the author, June 24, 1989.
7 Greenhous and Hillmer, p. 140.
8 *PAC*, Records of the Royal Canadian Air Force, RG 24, Vol. 5265, File HQS 25–3–3, *No. 32 S.F.T.S.—Disturbances—*, Memorandum of L. S. Breader, Chief of the Air Staff to the Minister, Aug. 4, 1943, paragraph 5–6.
9 *Ibid.*, paragraph 2–4.
10 *PAC*, RG 24, Vol. 5265, File HQS 25–3–3, Copy of a Minute of Air Council on Wednesday, July 28, 1943, paragraphs 172 and 207. See also, *PAC*, RG 24, Vol. 5265, File HQS 25–3–3, Extract from Air Force Routine Orders Dated 11th June, 1943, paragraphs 1–6.
11 *PAC*, RG 24, Vol. 5265, File HQS 25–3–3, Memorandum by L. W. Marlor, Deputy Assistant Provost Marshal, No. 4 Training Command, Aug. 3, 1943, paragraph 2.
12 *Ibid.*, paragraph 20.
13 *Ibid.*, paragraphs 9–16.
14 *PAC*, RG 24, Vol. 5265, File HQS 25–3–3A, *City of Moose Jaw, Sask.—Disturbances at—*, Memorandum by L. W. Marlor, Deputy Assistant Provost Marshal, No. 4 Training Command, Sept. 13 [18?], 1944, paragraph 7.
15 *Ibid.*, paragraph 6.
16 *PAC*, RG 24, Vol. 5265, File HQS 25–3–3A, Memorandum by A. Woodward, Division "F" RCMP, Sept. 14, 1944, paragraph 5.
17 *PAC*, RG 24, Vol. 5265, File HQS 25–3–3A, Memorandum by L. W. Marlor, Deputy Assistant Provost Marshal, No. 4 Training Command, Sept. 13 [18?], 1944, paragraph 6.
18 *PAC*, RG 24, Vol. 5265, File HQS 25–3–3A, Memorandum by Assistant Commissioner Commanding "F" Division RCMP, Regina to Commissioner of the RCMP, Ottawa, Oct. 18, 1944, paragraph 4.
19 *PAC*, RG 24, Vol. 5265, File HQS 25–3–3A, Memorandum by A. Woodward, Division "F" RCMP, Sept. 14, 1944, paragraph 5.
20 *PAC*, RG 24, Vol. 5265, File HQS 25–3–3A, Memorandum by Constable H.S. Hilts, Moose Jaw City Police to The Chief Constable, Moose Jaw City Police, Sept. 14, 1944.
21 *PAC*, RG 24, Vol. 5265, File HQS 25–3–3A, Memorandum by L.W. Marlor, Deputy Assistant Provost Marshal, No. 4 Training Command, Sept. 13 [18?], 1944, paragraph 8.
22 *Ibid.*, paragraph 10.
23 "All Quiet on the Moose Jaw Front Wednesday Night," *The Moose Jaw Times-Herald*, Sept. 14, 1944, p. 5.
24 *PAC*, RG 24, Vol. 5265, File HQS 25–3–3A, Memorandum by Assistant Commissioner Commanding "F" Division RCMP, Regina to Commissioner of the RCMP, Ottawa, Oct. 18, 1944, paragraph 5.
25 *PAC*, RG 24, Vol. 5265, File HQS 25–3–3A, Memorandum by L. W. Marlor, Deputy Assistant Provost Marshal, No. 4 Training Command, Sept. 13 [18?], 1944, paragraphs 11–12.
26 *Ibid.*, paragraph 5.
27 *PAC*, RG 24, Vol. 5265, File HQS 25–3–3A, Memorandum by A. Woodward, Division "F" RCMP, Sept. 14, 1944, paragraph 2.
28 *PAC*, RG 24, Vol. 5265, File HQS 25–3–3A, Memorandum by L. W. Marlor, Deputy Assistant Provost Marshal, No. 4 Training Command, Sept. 13 [18?], 1944, paragraph 5.
29 *PAC*, RG 24, Vol. 5265, File HQS 25–3–3A, Memorandum by Air Vice Marshal, RAF Liaison Officer, Ottawa, to The Deputy Commissioner RCMP, Ottawa, October 14, 1944, paragraph 2(a); Memorandum by Assistant Commissioner Commanding "F" Division RCMP, Regina to Commissioner of the RCMP, Ottawa, Oct. 18, 1944, paragraph 2.
30 Greenhous and Hillmer, p. 141; *PAC*, RG 24, Vol. 5265, File HQS 25–3–3A, Memorandum by A. Woodward, Division "F" RCMP, Sept. 14, 1944, paragraphs 1–4.

31 *PAC*, RG 24, Vol. 5265, File HQS 25–3–3A, Memorandum by Assistant Commissioner Commanding "F" Division RCMP, Regina to Commissioner of the RCMP, Ottawa, Oct. 18, 1944, paragraph 6.

32 *PAC*, RG 24, Vol. 5265, File HQS 25–3–3A, Memorandum by Air Vice Marshal, RAF Liaison Officer, Ottawa, to The Deputy Commissioner RCMP, Ottawa, Oct. 14, 1944.

33 *PAC*, RG 24, Vol. 5265, File HQS 25–3–3A, Memorandum by H. F. Gordon, Deputy Minister to the Commissioner, RCMP, Ottawa Oct. 21, 1944.

34 Interview: Roland Wilkes with the author, June 24, 1989.

Notes for Chapter 12

A Crisis of its Own

1 Rivers, *The Gazette*, Jan. 30, 1941.
2 Virden, *The Empire-Advance*, Nov. 20, 1940.
3 *Weyburn Review*, Dec. 18, 1941.
4 *The Neepawa Press*, Nov. 5, 1942.
5 Canada, *Canada Year Book 1942* (Ottawa: King's Printer, 1942), p. 84.
6 Saskatoon *Star Phoenix*, Sept. 12, 1940.
7 Swift Current, *Sun*, April 28, 1942.
8 *The Assiniboia Times*, Aug. 19, 1942.
9 *The Selkirk Record*, July 29, 1943.
10 Rivers, *The Gazette*, July 17, 1941.
11 Swift Current *Sun*, Aug. 31, 1943.
12 *The Edmonton Journal*, Aug 27, 1940.
13 Interview: Phil Ellison with the author, June 7, 1989.
14 Letter: Bill Hemstreet to the author, Nov. 17, 1986.
15 *The Assiniboia Times*, July 24, 1985.
16 Interview: Ken Melby with author, Dec. 28, 1987.
17 Interview: J. P. Kirk with author, Sept. 29, 1987.
18 Virden, *The Empire-Advance*, April 25, 1945.
19 Interview: A. S. Edger with author, Aug. 5 1987.
20 Interview: Phil Ellison with the author, June 7, 1989.
21 Interview: Ken Currie with the author, June 8, 1989.
22 *Ibid.*
23 Saskatoon, *Star Phoenix*, Sept. 5, 1940.
24 *The Calgary Herald*, Sept. 25, 1940.
25 *The Winnipeg Tribune*, June 21, 1941.
26 Interview: A. S. Edger with author, Aug. 5, 1988.
27 Interview: Phil Ellison with the author, June 7, 1989.
28 *The Estevan Mercury*, Aug. 6, 1942.
29 *Weyburn Review*, Sept. 3, 1942.
30 Letter: Bill Hemstreet to the author, Nov. 17, 1986.
31 Interview: Jim Kirk with the author, Sept. 29, 1987.
32 *Yorkton Enterprise*, July 2, 1942; May 7, 1942; Swift Current *Sun*, Sept. 15, 1942; Letter: Dorothy Minor to the author, Feb. 26, 1987.
33 Swift Current *Sun*, Oct. 6, 1942.
34 Dafoe, No. 5 B&GS *Diary*, Aug. 12, 1942.
35 *Reflection by the Quills* (Wynyard: Quill Historical Society, 1981), p. 685.
36 *Davidson Leader*, Feb. 10, 1943; Town of Davidson Council Minutes, July 4, 1940.

Notes for Chapter 13

Mackenzie King, Diefenbaker, and the Struggle for a School

1 Fred Hatch, "Mackenzie King And No. 6 Air Observer School" (An unpublished paper), pp. 2–4.

2 *Ibid.*

3 *Queen's University Archives* [hereafter *QUA*], Power Papers, file D1074, note initialled by H. R. Stewart, Air Secretary, Oct. 9, 1940.

4 *Ibid.*, Power to Curror, Jan 8, 1941; Order in Council PC 1329, Feb. 24, 1941; Hatch, "Mackenzie King And No. 6 Air Observer School," p. 5.

5 *PAC* MG 26, J4, King Papers, "Memorandum re Prince Albert Air Observer School," June 1942.

6 Hatch, "Mackenzie King And No. 6 Air Observer School," p. 7.

7 *PAC* MG 26, J4, King Papers, "Memorandum re Prince Albert Air Observer School," June 1942.

8 Hatch, "Mackenzie King And No. 6 Air Observer School," p. 8.

9 *Ibid.*; *PAC* MG 26, J4, King Papers, "Memorandum re Prince Albert Air Observer School," June 1942; *QUA*, Power Papers, Department of National Defense For Air Development Committee, Minutes, May 5, 1942, Paragraphs 36–38.

10 *PAC* MG 26, J4, King Papers, "memorandum re Prince Albert Air Observer School," June 1942; John A. Munroe and J.H. Archer, eds., *One Canada: Memoirs of the Right Honourable John G. Diefenbaker. The Crusading Years 1895–1956* (Toronto: Macmillan, 1975), pp. 145–167; Canada, House of Commons, *Debates*, April 30, 1942.

11 *PAC* MG 26, J4, King Papers, "Memorandum re Prince Albert Air Observer School," June 1942.

12 *QUA*, Power Papers, King to Power, June 23, 1942.

13 *Ibid*, Power to King, June 24, 1942.

14 *Ibid.*, King to Power, July 1, 1942.

15 *Ibid.*, Power to King, July 7, 1942, Hatch, "Mackenzie King And No. 6 Air Observer School," p. 11.

16 Hatch, "Mackenzie King And No. 6 Air Observer School," p. 11.

17 *QUA*, Power Papers, King to Power, July 23, 1942.

18 Hatch, "Mackenzie King And No. 6 Air Observer School," p. 12.

19 *QUA*, Power Papers, King to Power, Aug. 21, 1942.

20 Hatch, "Mackenzie King And No. 6 Air Observer School," p. 13.

21 *Public Archives of Saskatchewan*, R-73 Mayson Papers, file 4.

22 *Department of National Defence, Directorate of History*, File 73/1558 v. 6, Meetings of the Supervisory Board of the BCATP, Reports of the Chief of the Air Staff, Aug. 17, to Oct. 19, 1942, Appendix "A"; Hatch, "Mackenzie King And No. 6 Air Observer School," p. 15.

23 Saskatoon, *Star Phoenix*, June 12, 1942; Hatch, "Mackenzie King And No. 6 Air Observer School," p. 15.

Notes for Chapter 14
The Plan's Aviation Legacy

1 *The Estevan Mercury*, Feb. 17, 1944.

2 *The North Battleford Optimist*, March 22, 1945.

3 Greenhous and Hillmer, p. 143.

4 Philip Smith, *It Seems Like Only Yesterday: Air Canada, the First 50 Years* (Toronto: McClelland and Stewart, 1986), p. 83.

Index

Aero Club of British Columbia, 1–2
Aerodrome Development Committee, 86
Air Cadets, see Cadets
Airspeed Oxford, 10
American Army Air Corp, 85
Apedaile, J. L., 88–89
Armistice (of the Great War), 2
Assiniboia, Sask., 11, 13, 51, 68, 75, 77
Athabaska, Alta., 92
Australia, 1, 4–5, 13, 57–58, 63, 90
Avro Anson, 10, 26, 36

Bands (musical), 55
Baseball, 58, 65–67
Basketball, 64
Beatty, Sir Edward, 16–17
Belgians, 13, 27, 90
Bennett, R. B., 3
Bingo, 58
Bowden, Alta., 11, 13
Boxing, 62
Brandon, Man., 11, 18, 56, 61, 66, 73
Bristol Bolingbrokes, 10
British Columbia Aviation School, see Aero Club of British Columbia

Cadets, 59
Calgary, Alta., 10–11, 13–15, 19, 27, 30, 63, 65, 76, 78–79
Canadian Airways, 84, 92
Canadian Expeditionary Forces, 1
Canadian Flying Clubs Association, 9
Canadian National Railway, 16–17, 90
Canadian Pacific Airlines, 92
Canadian Pacific Railways, 16–17, 38
Canadian Women's Army Corp, see Women's Division (RCAF)
Carberry, Man., 11, 13, 55, 62–63, 73
Caron, Sask., 11, 13, 66, 77
Cessna Cranes, 10
Chamberlain, Neville, 4–5
Claresholm, Alta, 11, 52–54, 57, 64, 81
Collins, Robert, 41
Co-operative Commonwealth Federation (CCF), 16
Cricket, 63–64, 68
Croil, Air Vice-Marshal G. M., 8
Curtiss Aviation School (Toronto), 1
Czechoslovakians, 13, 27, 90

Dafoe, Sask., 11, 43, 51, 53, 56, 81
Dances, 56–58
Dauphin, Man., 11, 77, 81
Davidson, Sask., 11, 19, 54–55, 64, 66, 81–82, 86–89
Denmark, 12
Department of National Defence, 2–3, 8, 15
Department of Transport, 8
Depression (Great), 4, 7, 14, 23, 27, 81
DeWinton, Alta., 11, 13
Diefenbaker, John G., 86–89
Drama, 53–55
Duncan, James S., 8
Dutch, 13, 27, 90

Edmonton, Alta., 11, 15, 18, 30, 65, 76, 78–79, 85
Egypt, 2
Estevan, Sask., 11, 13, 15, 20, 41, 55, 61–62, 66, 79–80, 90

Fairchild Cornell, 10
Fairey Battles, 10
Films, 52–53
Fleet Finch, 10
Floud, Sir Frances, 2–3
Fort Fleet, 10
France, 12
Free French, 13, 27, 90
Flin Flon, Man., 65

Greenhous, Brereton, 58–59, 69
George, Group Captain, 69–70
Germany, 4, 8, 39, 89
Gimili, Man., 11
Godfrey, Group Captain A. F., 4
Golf, 61
Great War, 1–2, 39, 83
Ground crew, 41–48; kitchen staff, 41; fire department, 43; motor transport, 43; meteorology, 45; maintenance, 45–48

Harvard, 10, 26
Hatch, Fred, 30
Hickes, Wing Commander H. V., 4
High River, Alta., 11
Hillmer, Norman, 58–59, 69
Hockey, 58, 64–65
Hostess clubs, 51–52
Humboldt, Sask., 56
Hurricane, 10

India (Indians training in Canada), 13, 27, 90

Index

King, William Lyon Mackenzie, 1–8, 26, 83–89

Lancaster (bomber), 48
Leckie, Group Captain Robert, 2
Lethbridge, Alta., 11, 18–19, 21, 58, 76, 79
Library, 51
Lysander, see Westland Lysander

MacDonald, Man., 11, 61
Mackenzie, Ian, 2
Maclachan, K. S., 8
Macleod, Alta., 11, 15, 18–19, 36, 38–39, 64
Maple Creek, Sask., 19
Mart Kenny and His Western Gentlemen, 57
Mayson and Campbell Aviation, 83–89, 92
McConnachie (Edmonton), 84–85
Medicine Hat, Alta., 11, 13, 15, 19, 65, 76
Meighen, Arthur, 3
Melfort, Sask., 56
Melville, Sask., 15–16
Moose Jaw, Sask., 11, 13, 15, 23–26, 55, 64–65, 67–72, 77, 79, 85
Mornison, N. E., 69
Mossbank, Sask., 11, 43, 51–52, 55, 62, 66, 71, 77, 79

Neepawa, Man., 11, 13, 38, 54, 62, 66, 74
New Zealand, 1, 4–5, 13, 57–58, 90
North Battleford, Sask., 11, 13, 15, 23–24, 53, 55, 58, 68, 90–91
North-West Staging Route, 85
Norway (Norwegians in Canada), 12–13, 27, 90

Oxford, see Airspeed Oxford

Parties, 52
Paulson, Man., 11, 54
Pearce, Alta., 11, 13, 19, 36, 39–40
Penhold, Alta., 11, 13, 15, 54, 63
Polish (airmen in Canada), 13, 27, 90
Portage la Prairie, Man., 11, 30, 43, 57
Power, C. G. ("Chubby"), 8, 38, 87–89
Prairie Airways (of Moose Jaw), 84, 92
Prince Albert, Sask., 11, 14, 26, 30, 52, 65, 83–89

Quebec, 3

Ralston, J. L., 5
Regina, Sask., 11, 14, 18, 20, 30, 40, 65, 68–69, 71, 85
Rivers, Man., 11, 18, 21–22, 36–37, 59, 61–63, 73, 76
Riversdale, Lord, 5
Rosetown, Sask., 15
Royal Canadian Mounted Police (North West Mounted Police), 38, 71, 77
Royal Flying Corp, 2
Royal Naval Air Corp, 2

St. Thomas, Ont., 30, 41
Saskatchewan Government Airways, 89
Saskatoon, Sask., 11, 14, 19, 26, 55, 61–62, 64–65, 68, 75, 78, 83
Selkirk, Man., 75
Shearer, Air Commodore, 85–86
Soccer, 63
Souris, Man., 11, 16–17, 49, 56, 61
Spitfire, 48
Stearman, 40
Stedman, Air Commodore E. W., 5
Swift Current, Sask., 11, 13, 22–23, 37, 51–52, 59–60, 63, 66, 75–76, 81
Swimming, 43, 61–62
Swinton, Lord, 2

Tedder, Group Captain Arthur (Marshal RAF, Lord Tedder), 2
Tennis, 63
Tiger Moth, 10
Track and field, 62–63
Trained in Canada scheme, 2–4
Trans-Canada Air Lines, 18, 92

United States of America, 2, 4, 14, 22, 57

Vancouver, BC, 19, 64, 68
Victoria, BC, 64, 68
Virden, Man., 11, 18–19, 73, 77
Visiting Forces Acts (1933), 13
Vulcan, Alta., 11, 18, 36

War Emergency Training Program, 27
Wardair, 92
Wartime Prices and Trade Board, 78, 81–82
Watson, Sask., 56
Weir, J. G., 2–3
Westland Lysanders, 10
Weyburn, Sask., 11, 13, 21, 23, 40, 60, 68, 74, 80
Wilson, J. A., 8
Winnipeg, Man., 11, 14, 18, 20, 30, 40, 49, 55, 62, 64–65, 73, 79, 85
Women's Division, RCAF, 46–48, 59, 64, 66
Wood, Sir Kingsly, 3
Wrestling, 62
Wynyard, Sask., 19

Yorkton, Sask., 11, 15, 26, 37, 43, 46, 49, 51, 55, 58, 65, 68, 78, 81
Yukon Southern Air Transport, 84